The Old Stones of Kingston

OL

Margaret Angus

PHOTOGRAPHS BY G. E. O. LILLEY

THE
TONES
OF KINGSTON

Its Buildings before 1867

UNIVERSITY OF TORONTO PRESS

© University of Toronto Press, 1966
Toronto   Buffalo   London
Printed in Canada
Reprinted, 1970, 1974
Reprinted in paperback, 1980, 1984
ISBN 0-8020-6419-1

Acknowledgments

THIS BOOK is the result of almost twenty years' spare-time research. The late Professor R. G. Trotter of Queen's University aroused my interest in the history of Kingston and pointed out the wealth of material available. The resulting search has led me into public and private archives and into the lives of some fascinating people. I have strained my eyes over delicate fading script and my back lifting great volumes of early newspapers.

I am especially indebted to some friends who share my interest in early Kingston and whose professional abilities have guided my study. Professor R. A. Preston, formerly of the Royal Military College at Kingston, has shared most generously his knowledge, his time and his enthusiasm. H. Pearson Gundy, former Librarian at Queen's University, has with gracious and enduring interest encouraged my searches, making easily available the fine resources of the Douglas Library through his most co-operative staff. Charles Beer, former Archivist at the Douglas Library, responded with suggestions to my every query and shared my excitement at even the small discoveries. Professor S. F. Wise of Queen's University also read the manuscript and made some very helpful suggestions.

I was fortunate in working with George Muirhead, former Planning Officer of Kingston, in the Committee for the Preservation of Buildings of Architectural and Historical Value. Over the few years of the committee's existence we compiled a great deal of information on Kingston's architectural heritage and framed a by-law which may some day protect that heritage.

Anthony Adamson and Marion MacRae are responsible for my interest in architectural history but not for any errors I have made in judgment or fact regarding Kingston architecture.

I am grateful to James Nielson whose organization of the archives in Kingston City Hall has made valuable records easily available.

My thanks go to the descendants of early Kingston families who loaned me family papers and took a lively interest in my work. I acknowledge also the interest of colleagues in the Kingston Historical Society and in the Architectural Conservancy of Ontario.

I have been assisted by grants from the Arts Research Committee of Queen's University. I am obliged to D. K. Grace who drew the maps and the doorway of Cartwright House, and to Norma McIlreath who typed and retyped these pages.

The artistry of George Lilley, who took all the contemporary photographs and copied the old ones in this book, is evident. For his interest and patience I shall always be grateful.

The research for and writing of this book have at times seriously disrupted our family life but my husband has encouraged me with sympathetic understanding and a cheerful disregard for domestic neglect.

M.A.

In the 1974 reprint, the three new photographs of buildings that have been restored—the City Hall, Wilson's Buildings, and Bellevue House—were taken by Wallace R. Berry.

M.A.

Contents

ACKNOWLEDGMENTS, v

Aerial photograph of market triangle, 2

INTRODUCTION, 3

Key map of Kingston, 4–5

Drawing of Cartwright House doorway by D. K. Grace, 10

THE OLD CITY, 19

Kingston City Hall, 20

St. George's Anglican Cathedral, 24

Gildersleeve House, 26

Plymouth Square, 28

Commercial Mart, 30

Wilson's Buildings, 30

Mowat's Round Corner Building, 30

OLD SYDENHAM WARD, 37

Cartwright House, 38

Earl Place, 40

Charles Place, 42

Edgewater, 44

THE FIRST SUBDIVISIONS, 48

St. Mary's Roman Catholic Cathedral, 50

Mowat Houses, 52

Elizabeth Cottage, 54

St. Andrew's Manse, 56

Frontenac County Court House, 58

McIntosh Castle, 60

Rosemount, 62

Earl Street houses, 155–169, 62

Sydenham Street United Church, 68

FARM LOT 24, 73

Murney Tower, 74

Kingston General Hospital, 76

Summerhill, 78

THE SHORE ROAD, 83

Hales Cottages, 84

Bellevue House, 86

vii

Roselawn, 88

St. Helen's, 90

Alwington House, 92

NORTH KINGSTON, 96

Kingston Brewery, 98

Barrack Street between Wellington
 and Rideau, 100

110 Rideau Street, 102

ACROSS THE RIVER, 106

St. Mark's Church, 108

The Stone Frigate, 110

Fort Henry, 112

BIBLIOGRAPHY, 114

INDEX, 117

The Old Stones of Kingston

2

Introduction

STILL VISIBLE AND TANGIBLE in the streets and environs of Kingston is the evidence of its place in the architecture and history of Canada. It is remarkably fortunate in having more old stone buildings than any other city of its size in Ontario. Many of these are homes, large or small; some are commercial buildings; still others are public buildings with a variety of uses.

Many of Kingston's older streets are lined with houses built of stone, and even in the new subdivisions there are old limestone farm houses, now surrounded by modern split-level dwellings. The highways leading into the city pass innumerable homesteads worthy of unhurried appreciation. Yet these old family dwellings, both in and out of the city, have become for most passers by just part of the landscape, and it is rare to find a local resident who can identify even the most notable of the early homes.

The number of early stone commercial buildings still in use is unusually large in Kingston. In the old business section near the lake—lower Princess Street, Brock Street and Ontario Street—many rugged survivors still stand. Most of them, however, have been so altered by fashion or "progress" that the only mark of their age or original architecture is in the upper storeys, which have so far escaped extensive alteration on the outside but which seldom attract from busy shoppers the upward look of admiration due the beauty of their weathered limestone.

Stone was also used almost exclusively in the first half of the nineteenth century for Kingston's churches, civic buildings and military installations, and its distinctive blue-grey tone gave added reason for the name, the Limestone City.

Some of these old buildings are noteworthy as architectural specimens,

3

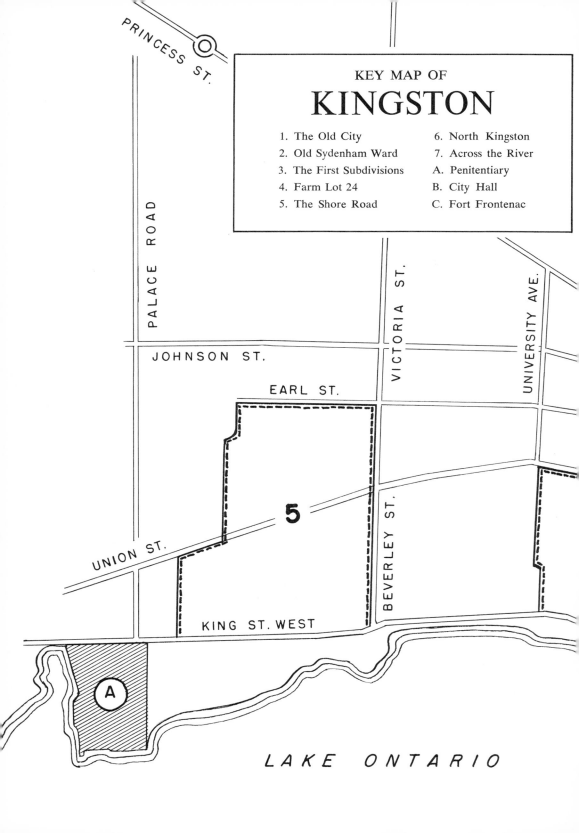

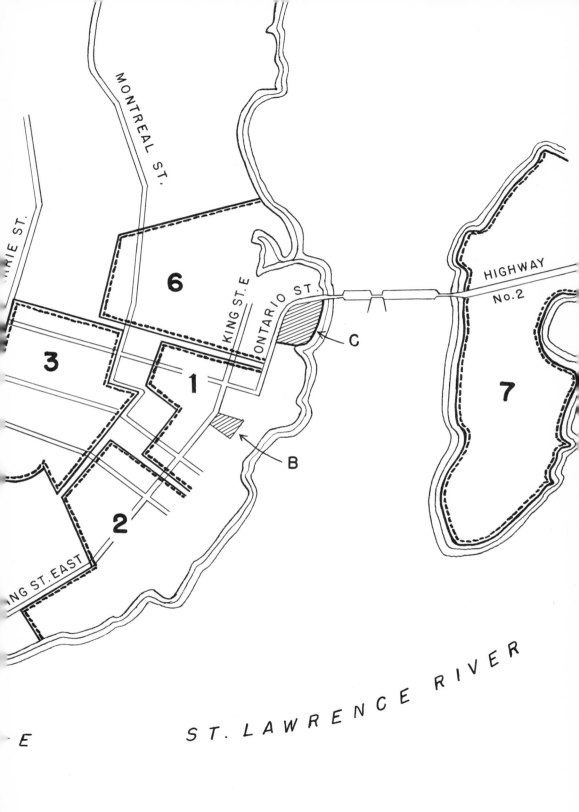

and many of them, now crowded tight by other buildings, once stood on beautiful sites where the lines and balance of their structure could show to advantage. But they all, regardless of their present situation, also kindle our interest because of what they have to tell us about the origins and way of life of the people who built them, the human story connected with them. They gave us a richer appreciation of the past as a vital part of the present and of the relation between the Kingston area and the country as a whole.

The pictures in this book represent the best choice which it proved possible to make of buildings erected before 1867 that would show Kingston's place in Canadian architecture, and the stories that accompany them will, it is hoped, tell of Kingston's place in the history of the country— political, economic and social. It has not been easy to make a final selection.

The choice has been dictated partly by irreparable losses. Terrible and uncontrollable fires destroyed many of the earliest buildings, which were then replaced by limestone or brick structures with thick, high firewalls. Others of the earliest buildings, strong candidates for inclusion by reason of their quaint personality or beauty or historical importance, have been destroyed to make way for commerce and industry: for example, one of the houses brought over from Carleton Island in 1783 to help house the Loyalists was replaced in 1928 by a gas station, and a beautiful stone house built in 1820 was replaced in 1956 by a supermarket.

Then also the choice has often had to be governed by the amount of data available. Moreover, strict architectural classification is not only difficult but in many cases impossible. Later changes or additions, unfortunately all too conspicuous, have often obliterated an original design beyond classification.

The story here recorded begins with the coming of the British settlers and the birth of a new province. It closes with Confederation, Canada's political coming of age.

The first building of any note erected in the Kingston area was a fort built by Count Frontenac in 1673. This was the first of a succession of forts on approximately the same site—some wooden, some stone. The present Fort Frontenac dates back only to 1843, but some recent excavations have laid bare a few foundations and steps of earlier forts. These are the only known remnants in Kingston of the period of French occupation.

British settlement in this area began in 1784 with the influx of the United Empire Loyalists, voluntary exiles from the new-born United States. The great majority of them had lost all except what they could carry—

their homes and lands had been confiscated. They came in large companies from New York City by sea to the Maritimes and up the St. Lawrence River, or in smaller, often family, groups north on Lake Champlain and across to the north shore of the St. Lawrence. In Canada they were assembled in camps until the government decided where to settle them and what supplies could be spared for them. They were the displaced persons of eighteenth-century America. Disbanded soldiers, attracted by offers of free land, followed the Loyalists and tended to settle together in communities near their former officers.

Some preparations had been made to receive the Loyalists at Kingston—or Cataraqui, as it was then called. Surveyors had marked out a townsite and divided into farm lots the near-by land along the lake front. Five buildings had been brought by raft from the naval base at Carleton Island, in the channel south of Wolfe Island near the American shore. At least two of these buildings were private property and had been used by merchants as both place of business and home. Only these and the partially rebuilt fort stood on the wooded shore where the settlers landed. They drew for town and farm lots and set to work.

Many of the settlers had never worked with logs before, so their first houses, which were in any case built hastily with inadequate tools, were mere shelters, bearing little resemblance to their former homes. Not until the land was cleared and better materials and tools were available could they build better houses. The first sawmills, operated free for the benefit of the settlers, barely supplied shingles for roofing and boards for flooring, doors and window-casings. The Reverend John Stuart wrote in 1786 from that early Kingston: "We live far removed from the great world. . . . everyone here is busied in procuring the necessaries of life, in cultivating land, building houses &c. . . ." In 1788 he wrote that "the town has upwards of 40 houses."

Most of those forty houses were clustered around Fort Frontenac, for Kingston, though small, was even then an important military settlement by virtue of its strategic location. It was thus set apart from other pioneer communities and had some reason to suppose it might become the capital of the upper province. Indeed it was in Kingston, on July 8, 1792, that Governor Simcoe proclaimed his government. But he soon moved on, with this government, to the western end of Lake Ontario. By that time, according to Mrs. Simcoe's account, Kingston had fifty houses—only one of which was built of stone.

Although Kingston did not become the capital of the new province, its geographical position at the junction of the St. Lawrence River and Lake Ontario not only ensured its continuance as a military garrison and naval base, but also made it a commercial port. It attracted new settlers, of course, and grew in size and significance. But for men and goods that merely passed through, it was a natural communication link between Montreal and the growing settlements in the western part of the province, including York (now Toronto). Thus the growth in shipping kept pace with the growth in settlement and vice versa. Soon the primitive log shanties were being improved upon. For instance, a 1791 Ordnance report tells of "weatherboarding the new store-house and guardhouse as well to preserve them as to prevent the annual expense of pointing &c." Another report, stating that "the shell of log work is in tolerable order," presents an estimate "for weatherboarding it and new shingling the roof both of which are very necessary."

By 1795 Kingston was said to have a hundred and thirty houses, a sizable community, but it had practically nothing of Limestone City about it. The Duc de la Rochefoucauld-Liancourt, who made the estimate, wrote, "if bricklayers could be procured even from Montreal . . . building with stone could be less expensive than with wood." Limestone was available; of that there was no doubt. It was only too evident to the settler using his plough. But building with stone required trained masons. At the beginning of the 1800s, buildings of weatherboard or roughcast over logs, or of frame with rubble fill between the walls, greatly outnumbered stone buildings.

The building area then reached out along the waterfront on both sides of the Fort—north along the Cataraqui River and around the present harbour area. More respectable stone structures began to replace the earlier buildings. A larger community, made up mostly of shop-and-home accommodations, spread out where today new commerce and industry have crowded the area.

As the settlement increased in size, building had to be carried beyond the fringe along the waterfront. This expansion, however, was cautious: by 1812 its farthest reach was seldom more than three blocks from the wharves. There was some building on the roads that led into the town, and larger houses replaced the first shelters on many of the pioneer farms in the immediate vicinity of Kingston. But during the ten years preceding the War of 1812, development, though steady, was gradual. No great change took place. Kingston was still a small village.

The War of 1812 promoted Kingston to the status of a major naval

8

base and military centre, but the sharp stimulus given to trade was its main contribution. The extension of settlement throughout the province made it necessary to import more goods, and there was a rise in the export of potash, lumber and wheat. Kingston, which could build boats either for war or for trade, and could act as a port of trans-shipment from lake boats to the smaller river boats, enjoyed a new prosperity. When the war was over, the shipbuilders concentrated on commercial vessels, and the general but temporary financial depression that came to Upper Canada with peace scarcely affected Kingston. Activity at the port continued and soon increased.

Greater activity in the port meant greater, and more substantial, building activity in the town and in the navy and army establishments. This included many dwellings for the growing population: by 1824 there were said to be four hundred and fifty homes in Kingston. The needs of religion, business and education were being met also. And for all these Kingston began to build for the future with something sturdier and more permanent than logs and weatherboarding. In the decade after the war, there appeared in the public press an increasing number of calls for tenders, mostly specifying stone. A very few builders did use brick, but in 1816 a brick building was so unusual and distinctive that it could serve as a sort of landmark. For instance, the circulating library announced the location of its new premises as on Store Street (now Princess) "opposite the brick building." In December 1816 there was the first call for tenders to build a stone house 200 feet by 80 feet in the naval yard at Point Frederick. Kingston no longer has a naval yard but the so-called Stone Frigate, finished in 1820, still stands on the grounds of the Royal Military College. In November 1816 the British Methodists called for tenders for "a chapel to be erected near the North Gate," the gate near Bay Street in the fortifications built around the town in 1812. St. George's Anglican Church, in spite of the addition of a second gallery, was too small for its congregation: even Lieutenant-Colonel Foster, Assistant Adjutant General, had to advertise "to purchase or rent a pew or seat." One business announced its removal to "an elegant new brick house in the main street" and another to "a new stone building." A school "lately in Mr. Henry Baker's Red House, Rear Street" (now Bagot), announced its removal to "the commodious Stone House . . . fronting Store Street . . . with a handsome paved play ground."

This growth of Kingston paralleled the growth in population and prosperity that began everywhere in Upper Canada after the brief post-war depression had passed. There was a tremendous surge of immigration that

Doorway - Cartwright House

D. K. GRACE · 1961

brought with it not only benefits but difficulties. Kingston had to endure cholera epidemics and grapple with the social problems posed by orphans and paupers.

Recognizing the importance of her rapidly expanding settlements in Canada, Britain took steps to keep them secure and protected. Extensive plans were made to fend off the Yankees, and for the next twenty years there was much defence construction at this point on what was to become in the next century the "undefended border." In the spring of 1827, contracts were let for the building of the Rideau Canal, an expensive work of great magnitude whose purpose was to allow boats to ply between Montreal and Kingston without having to sail under the barrels of American guns along the St. Lawrence. In May, work began on the Kingston Mills locks, the ones nearest Kingston, and a steady stream of men and supplies began to flow into the busy port. The importance for Kingston's buildings was that many expert stone masons were attracted to the area by the prospect of working on the Canal. A typical newspaper advertisement of 1829 reads: "Wanted at Long Falls, South Crosby, on the Rideau Canal, about 20 stone masons to whom liberal encouragement will be given. MacKay and Redpath."

Other building in and around Kingston evidently gave "liberal encouragement" to "good stone masons" from 1827 to 1836. It was during this period that the second Fort Henry was rising on its point of land to the east of Kingston: the first Fort Henry, started in 1812, was not considered strong enough to protect this western end of the Rideau Canal. The Penitentiary was built on the lovely wooded shore of a small bay to the west of the town (far to the west as it seemed then) and the first prisoners were in its small, cold cells in 1835. That same year the General Hospital was completed but could not be put into use for lack of funds: the many benefactors who had contributed to the original hospital fund were putting their money into the building of their own residences in or near the town and employing those "good stone masons."

The early buildings with their purely functional style were now succeeded by Loyalist-style cottages of cut stone and by the more stately and elegant Georgian mansions with carefully proportioned façades. The formality in the placing of doors, windows and even wings was evidence that the appearance of buildings was being influenced by considerations of fashion and taste, as well as by wealth and higher standards of comfort. There were indeed a few professional architects in Kingston to guide the taste of the wealthy. Many of the builders, however, simply made use of designs from famous English and Scottish architects whose plans were then appearing in builders' guides. Others copied from memory the eighteenth-century domestic architecture they had admired at home in England or Scotland. A few Loyalists imitated styles that had been popular in the American colonies at the time of their emigration.

The one-storey stone cottage, built on a larger scale than its wooden predecessors, needed more light in the garret than the end gables could give. So that device typical of Ontario houses—the gable over the centre door—made its appearance. A wing was added to the back of the cottage when more space was needed. This type of dwelling was most popular on the outlying roads and farms where land was plentiful.

In town, houses with two storeys and a garret made better use of small lots. The beauty of the plain façades of these houses lies mainly in the size and symmetrical placing of the openings—a centre door, a window at either end and three windows in the second storey. The addition of a fan-light and side lights to the main doorway gave more light to the centre hallway and was usually balanced by making the centre window on the second storey more elaborate than the other two; sometimes it was a Palladian window. The stone houses built in Kingston from 1820 on have also the surface enrichment possible only in stone—the light and shadow brought out by rustication and the use of angle quoins. The grouping of chimney stacks also emphasized the balanced composition that marks the Georgian style. Some of the house fronts were varied by shallow, projecting pavilions rising the full height of the house and crowned with a pediment. Others had small porticos with columns and pilasters. Kingston was enjoying a period of prosperity; these mansions were visible evidence of that.

Elsewhere in Upper and Lower Canada political ferment and clamour for reform were leading to the Rebellion of 1837. Though Kingston was the home of some Family Compact members, it was perhaps prosperity rather than their presence that kept the area a conservative stronghold. With an economy based on trans-shipment, garrisons and defence construction, Kingston had few reasons for the complaints about government abuses that were rife in the western settlements of Upper Canada and in areas nearer by where an economy more typical of the frontier prevailed. A prosperous community where Loyalists and imperial troops, merchants and officials predominated was not likely to be a hotbed of unrest.

It was as a garrison town that Kingston felt the Rebellion. The imperial troops in Fort Henry were sent to the troubled area in Lower Canada, and the Canadian militia was called to garrison Kingston. When the alarms of the actual Rebellion were sounded and an attack on Kingston was expected momentarily, there was great military excitement. Kingston might need to be protected from the rebels who had attacked Toronto. Patrols were set up on the harbour ice to ward off forays by rebel sympathizers from the States. But there were no raids, and Fort Henry became merely the prison for the convicted rebels.

All this—the loyalty of the area, its garrisons and defences, its central position and its substantial stone buildings—soon brought Kingston to the political front. In 1841, Charles Poulett Thomson, Lord Sydenham, putting into effect the Durham Report which recommended the union of Upper and Lower Canada, chose Kingston to be the first capital. But as early as 1839, rumours of this possibility had increased land transfers and prices. Late in 1840 the tentative inquiries of government officials regarding buildings in Kingston had heightened the excitement.

On February 15, 1841, Lord Sydenham issued a proclamation summoning the new Parliament of Canada to meet in Kingston on May 26, 1841; the sitting was later postponed to June 14. On February 26 Sydenham had written in a confidential dispatch to the Colonial Secretary, Lord John Russell:

In pursuance of what I had the honour of stating upon a former occasion, I decided on calling the first Parliament at Kingston and of [sic] placing the seat of Government there. Upon investigation I found that I could obtain without difficulty the necessary accommodation both for the Legislature and the Government Offices, of a temporary nature, but still affording more convenience at less cost than if I had fixed upon either Montreal or Toronto. The Hospital which was recently erected, but has remained unoccupied, will, with slight alterations, afford better accommodation for the meeting of the Legislature than even at Toronto. I have hired a new range of buildings which was destined for warehouses and can be easily finished for their new purposes as Govt. Offices, for all the different Departments of the Government, and they will be far superior in convenience to any that are to be found in any of the Three Cities of the Province. I have hired a house for the Residence of the Governor-General, which with some additions will answer the purpose, and altho' the different Officers of the Government will be obliged to submit to inconveniences for a time, I have no doubt that accommodation can be provided. . . .

There was a frantic scurrying to find sufficient living accommodation for the immediate influx of people. The Kingston Board of Trade, threatened with government displeasure because of the housing shortage, appealed to the citizens. Those with suitable homes were urged to make them available or to share them with government officials. The Board of Works started contractors on the alterations of the buildings leased by the government, and a building boom was on.

For three years Kingston was the capital of Canada. In that time over four hundred homes were built for rental purposes. Commercial buildings were started in anticipation of an increase in business and the Town Council called for plans for a municipal building fit for a nation's capital. Queen's College opened classes in 1842 in a house on Colborne Street but had plans drawn up for buildings on ground it had acquired opposite the new Government House. The popular building area was along the lake shore toward the Parliament Building and the Governor General's Residence; but buildings were going up all over town.

Any period of greatly accelerated building yields some architectural oddities, and Kingston had its share. Yet the notable houses built in this period are mostly stone, conservative Georgian mansions, not very different from those built in the previous ten years. Some wood trim is a little coarser, and the window panes, though a bit bigger, are not so attractive.

As land prices rose, houses were built on smaller lots and the farm lots near Kingston were subdivided for home sites. Colonel Oldfield, Officer Commanding the Royal Engineers in Canada, in recommending the purchase of certain land in Kingston for extensive defence works, wrote in 1842, "such new buildings as have been erected since 1840 . . . have within the period of 2 years increased the value of the land by £1919. . . . At present the price of property rises and falls with the hopes and fears of the Kingston proprietors as to the future seat of government." They had reason for fear, since the majority of the politicians were not satisfied with Kingston as the seat of government and soon began manœuvres to move the capital. Rumours were plentiful, and a cautious few among the Kingstonians decided to wait and see before doing more building. Others with buildings under way had to finish them and hope for the best. In November 1843 the decision was made—Parliament was to meet next in Montreal.

The exodus began and depression hit Kingston. The newspapers were full of advertisements: houses for rent, houses for sale at greatly reduced prices. Some men went bankrupt and many suffered severe financial losses.

The few cautious ones who still had funds bought up quantities of valuable property at sacrifice prices.

But the departure of the government, the politicians and minor officials, did not crush Kingston completely. The commercial activity of its port and the plans for new military defences were bright spots in the economic outlook. During 1846 and 1847 the martello towers were built in the harbour, on Point Frederick, Cedar Island and Murney Point. The Market Battery (since torn down) also kept stone masons busy.

Kingston and its people moved with the times. Problems of health and comfort became public issues. Immigrants, continuing to pour into the country, brought the severe cholera epidemic of 1847. Emergency hospital facilities and nursing quarters were hastily put up. These brought some comfort to the sick and many irate protests to the City Council—from householders near these temporary buildings. The *Chronicle and News* of February 14, 1849, announced that John A. Macdonald had introduced in Parliament a bill to incorporate the City of Kingston Waterworks Company, and that the stock in it would be a good investment. The story continued,

Two-thirds of the city is now supplied with water for *all* household purposes by the carters—often from suspicious localities—and the other one-third from wells, which owing to the filtration through limestone, all are injurious to health —many of them brackish; whereas the Waterworks Company will supply the town with a pure article from the limpid Lake Ontario.

The increasing speed and ease of communication greatly influenced the prosperity and hence the building activity of Kingston. The opening of the western part of the province, with the traffic up river of men and supplies and the movement down river of grain, expanded the shipping trade, and the harbour was full and busy during the late forties and early fifties. In that period, there began in home-building a definite trend away from the commercial section of the city. Families who for years had lived over their places of business now moved to residential areas. The architectural style for big houses changed very little but there was a variety of styles in the more modest dwellings. Verandahs were added and the woodwork was a little more elaborate. Brick and stucco were becoming more popular but limestone was still used a great deal.

A serious threat to the city's prosperity as a port, and especially as a port of trans-shipment, came with the era of railroad-building. The growth of this rival transportation system made shipping interests, which had indulged in a period of over-expansion, look to plans for holding on to what business they had. In this struggle over methods of transportation Kingston managed to maintain its place as a port of trans-shipment for bulk cargoes of wheat; but the railroads gradually took over the smaller cargoes and the passengers.

Kingston's military importance seemed to be on the wane also. Compared to the dangers that were looming up in the Crimea, the threat of aggression at this North American border point was negligible, and in 1853 the British regiments were withdrawn. The garrison felt the loss of prestige and the city suffered too. Kingston society, which had always looked to the scarlet-coated officers for excitement, entertainment and an additional source of marriage prospects, was now thrown on its own resources. Houses were empty, calls for tenders for garrison supplies were drastically reduced, and the tavern keepers, of course, cut their orders to brewers and distillers. While the war lasted, only a few companies of Royal Canadian Rifles were stationed here. When the 9th Regiment returned to Kingston from the Crimea in 1856, the city rejoiced, and with good reason, but this return to the old ways was to last only a few years beyond Confederation—to 1871, when all the imperials were withdrawn from Canada.

In the meantime, industries were being set up all around Lake Ontario and Kingston managed to obtain a few minor ones—the lumber-forwarding business on Garden Island, two miles to the south, was claimed as a home industry. But the city continued to depend mainly on the trans-shipment of wheat, against the constant threat of the railroads and the difficulty of obtaining capital.

And of course Kingston continued to expand as a military centre—for it was still important in Canadian terms—and as an educational centre. This meant additions to existing public buildings and the erection of new ones, particularly churches and schools. What had been vacant lots were gradually filled with houses. The social texture of the community remained much the same, with a predominance of officials, military people and well-to-do merchants. Their substance, their strength and their quiet good taste were expressed in the material they most often chose for shelter, trade and worship, and when Confederation came in 1867 Kingston was a city built of stone.

The Old City

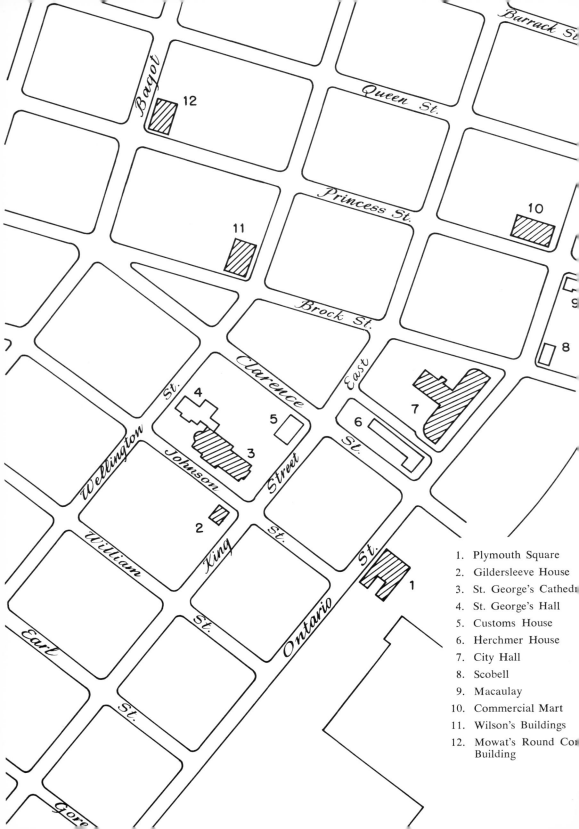

1. Plymouth Square
2. Gildersleeve House
3. St. George's Cathedr
4. St. George's Hall
5. Customs House
6. Herchmer House
7. City Hall
8. Scobell
9. Macaulay
10. Commercial Mart
11. Wilson's Buildings
12. Mowat's Round Cor
    Building

THE OLD CITY

SETTLEMENT in Kingston was not haphazard even at the beginning, because surveyor John Collins and his crew had laid out a townsite before the first settlers arrived. The street pattern was adapted to the shape of the waterfront by fitting a wedge between two grid plots. The wedge-shaped section (Brock to Clarence streets) was designated for a market and a church and soon became the centre or core around which the area now called the Old City developed. The lots reserved for a marketplace on the original plan are now the site of Kingston's City Hall—a magnificent site overlooking the harbour.

For over a century, Kingston was oriented to the waterfront. Building—public, commercial and domestic—was concentrated in a comparatively narrow strip near the water and along the main roads. The Post Office and Customs Department were conveniently close to wharves and storehouses. Hotels and inns clustered near the market. Banks and stores built where business was best.

The stone building at the southeast corner of Ontario and Princess streets was built by John Macaulay about 1829 as his residence and office when he was Postmaster. It was later occupied by the Bank of Upper Canada. One block south, on the northeast corner of Ontario and Brock, Richard Scobell built a large warehouse and dwelling in 1837. The present Customs House (built in 1856), at the southwest corner of King and Clarence, is on the site of the earliest Court House and Gaol.

The Herchmers had built on the corner of Ontario and Market streets before 1817. Behind their house the other buildings facing the market square were hotels built before 1853. The British American Hotel at King and Clarence streets (it was destroyed by fire in 1963) was Edward and Robert Walker's new hotel in 1807. Kingston assemblies were held there; Charles Dickens slept there; and on June 20, 1844, when Governor General Sir Charles Metcalfe left Kingston, it was there that he entertained local society at breakfast.

Today Kingston has spread its shopping centres, industry and subdivisions far beyond the waterfront, but the Old City area still has stores, offices and hotels and its government buildings, both federal and municipal.

Kingston City Hall

ONTARIO BETWEEN BROCK AND MARKET

The story of Kingston's City Hall covers Kingston's rise to prominence as capital of Canada, its sudden fall from favour and the long slow years of growth that followed.

In 1841, the Mayor, John Counter, and the other civic officials felt that Kingston should have a municipal building befitting its status as national capital. Plans were drawn by the architect, George Browne, money was borrowed, contracts were let and on June 5, 1843, the cornerstone was laid by the Governor General, Sir Charles Metcalfe.

The use planned for the building, as stated in a letter of 1843 to the *Chronicle and Gazette*, is a comment on the customs of the time. The basement fronting the water had fourteen offices meant for lawyers, brokers, etc.; behind these were to be the police establishment and the office of the clerk of the market. On the main floor, the north wing was to be the Post Office, with post boxes in the present Council Chamber, the south wing was for the Customs Department and the centre section was to contain the Corporation offices, five shops and a big newsroom. Upstairs would be the Town Hall for meetings and dances, and opposite it the Merchants' Exchange (Ontario Hall). The attic was to house the Mechanics' Institute and the dome their Library. The back wing, known as the Market Shambles, was to provide space for the green market and butchers' stalls and, in the King Street end, for

auction marts, printing offices and two eating houses. The building was obviously meant to be a real centre of all municipal functions, social, political and economic.

The estimated cost was £19,500, but the estimates were exceeded from the very start. The town quarrelled with its architect, George Browne, and in March 1844 dismissed him and employed William Coverdale. When the building was finished the contractors' demands for extras brought the actual cost to £28,000. By that time the capital had left Kingston. The building had been offered to the government, rent free, to induce them to stay, but the offer had been refused. All over town, buildings were empty, businesses failed and tax returns fell. Every possible expedient was used in an effort to carry the interest on the municipal debt. The offer to the government was repeated in 1848 and again in 1854, but to no avail. For many years any extra space was rented: to saloons (at either end of the main part), banks, dry goods stores, printing offices and the Post Office and Customs Department, both of which stayed until 1859. Some of the offices in the basement were even rented as living quarters until the City was threatened with an increase in insurance premiums in May 1848. As late as February 1854 the minutes of City Council note repeated attempts to dispossess an Irishwoman who refused offers to provide her with a house and pay her moving expenses.

As the work and therefore the administrative staff of municipal government increased, the City gradually took over more and more of the building. Memorial Hall was established in the Town Hall room in 1921 as a tribute to the men of Kingston who died in the First World War. In 1946, further expansion made necessary the temporary division of the Merchants' Exchange into offices. The magnificent curved ceiling, coffered and panelled with eighteen centre flowers, is now hidden from view.

These were all deliberate changes, but there were also two drastic changes dictated by calamity. On January 10, 1865, fire destroyed the Market Shambles. At that time the back wing extended right to King Street, where it ended in a square three-storey structure surmounted by a clock tower and bell. After the fire the wing was reconstructed on a smaller scale. Then in 1955 a fault was discovered in the portico, which was removed in 1956. A false pediment was applied in 1963 to protect the stone work until the portico was restored in 1966.

The City Hall is one of the great classical buildings of Ontario and as such has been declared a Historic Site. The federal government provided funds for the restoration of the portico with its four great columns and classical pediment. The building is in the form of a T, its front, 250 feet wide, facing the harbour. Crowning the three-storey central block is a circular drum (30 feet in diameter) illuminated by sixteen windows. The drum supports a dome which has a clockface centred over every fourth window. Rising from the dome is a slender cupola. The height from the bottom of the drum to the top of the cupola is about fifty-five feet. The front wings of the building, two storeys in height, have decorative parapets at either end to add height. The end walls, curved toward the back wing, have four niches intended to hold statues of public men: they are still empty. The ground-floor windows in the front of the building are set in segmented arches and the second-storey windows are recessed in a shallow arcade.

Inside City Hall much of the classical trim is still intact. The two big halls on the second floor, both 96 feet long, 50 feet wide and 28 feet high, have pilasters, columns and rich entablatures supporting great curved and decorated ceilings. The dome, now closed to the public, has a beautiful stairway winding up to the cupola.

Both inside and out, the stone work and the treatment of door and window openings show the boldness and skill of the architect.

There are marked similarities to the Custom House, Dublin, Ireland, built in 1781–91 to the plans of James Gandon, architect.

Restored and renovated 1973 under the direction of Neil MacLennan, architect.

St. George's Anglican Cathedral

KING STREET EAST AT JOHNSON

St. George's Church was started in 1825 to replace a smaller church of the same name one block away which was built in 1792.

The first Church of England services in Kingston were held in a room in the Tête du Pont Barracks, the Reverend John Stuart, Chaplain to the Forces, officiating.

Dr. John Stuart's parish was to have a special place not only in the religious life of the province, but in the educational and civil life also. At first his charge covered all of Upper Canada, and he travelled throughout the province to white and Indian settlements alike. The first school in Kingston was his, and he encouraged free schools in other parts of the province. For some years all the baptisms, marriages and deaths that took place in Upper Canada were recorded in the parish registers of the Anglican churches; thus the Established Church became the repository for the records of all the denominations in the early settlements.

The Stuarts, father and son, were clergymen at St. George's from its beginning in 1792 to the death of Archdeacon George Okill Stuart in 1862. In March of that year St. George's became a Cathedral and the Reverend Dr. John Travers Lewis became the first Bishop of the Diocese of Ontario.

The first St. George's Church on this site was a rectangular building of stone built to the plans of Thomas Rogers. It was enlarged and the front was rebuilt in 1846 when the portico and clock tower were added in the Georgian style. In 1891, when the building was again greatly enlarged, a change was made in the style and a dome similar to that of St. Paul's in London added. In the restoration made necessary by the fire of January 1, 1899, which had completely gutted the interior, the architect, Joseph Power, improved his plans and made some additions. The Johnson Street portico was added and the dome and roof were covered with copper.

There are many tablets and memorials of historical interest in the Cathedral. Lord Sydenham, the first Governor General of Canada after the 1840 union of the provinces, is buried under the floor of the nave. The two galleries are reserved for the cadets of the Royal Military College and their colours hang in front of the right-hand gallery. The flags at the front of the Cathedral are the colours of several Canadian battalions who served in the two world wars.

The men's and boys' choir of St. George's Cathedral has gained international recognition for the quality of its music, and has sung in the great cathedrals of England and the United States.

24

Gildersleeve House

Henry Gildersleeve (1785–1851) came to Kingston from Gildersleeve, Connecticut, just after the War of 1812. He was a shipwright by trade, and found employment in a yard owned by a widow, Mrs. Finkle. His first work was on the *Frontenac*, the first steamship to navigate the Great Lakes. In 1818 he was able to start his own shipping line, and in 1824 he married Mrs. Finkle's daughter, Sarah. The names of Henry Gildersleeve, his sons and grandson, are associated with the development of steam navigation on Lake Ontario, especially in the Bay of Quinte region. Gildersleeve himself was President of the Kingston Marine Railway Company and, as early as 1846, a member of the Kingston and Toronto Railroad Committee. The family interest in transportation began when water was the main highway and ended in 1912 when it had been superseded by steel rails.

Henry Gildersleeve started his big stone house in 1825, a year after his wedding, and moved in late in 1826. The house is fine Loyalist-style ashlar with projecting corner quoins and four large chimneys. The façade has a shallow central projection crowned with a pediment, and a simple cornice forms pediments with small arched windows in the gable ends. The portico, side lights and elliptical fanlight of the wide doorway are balanced by the large window grouping in the second floor. The other windows in the upper front are four full panes and two half panes wide to keep a centre muntin.

The original kitchen, cistern, servants' rooms and wine cellar were in the basement. On the main floor the library was behind the drawing room and across the central hall were the dining room and the breakfast room. On the second floor folding doors could be opened to make two bedrooms into a ballroom, and when Overton Smith Gildersleeve was Mayor of Kingston in 1855–56 he gave an official banquet there. In those days there were servants to keep the panelled fireplaces stocked with wood, to polish the solid walnut doors and to look after the grandchildren who came to live in the big house.

A sunroom has been added, the lower front windows have been resashed, and some remnants of a former stuccoing remain; otherwise the house is little altered. The original stone and cast-iron fence still encloses the property but the stable and carriage house were rebuilt about 1890. At the edge of the street the old hitching post and carriage step still stand.

When Miss Lucretia Gildersleeve, Henry's eldest daughter, died in 1909 the house was sold to Dr. W. R. Glover, who lived there until 1962. It is now used as an office building, but is carefully maintained with a proper appreciation of its architectural and historical value.

Plymouth Square

ONTARIO STREET AT JOHNSON

This range of buildings, designed for a dwelling and commercial premises, was built about 1831–32 by John Counter, a rather striking example of an English immigrant who made good in commerce and in public life. In 1855, plagued by financial reverses and family sorrow, he retired into obscurity.

Counter is believed to have come to Kingston about 1820, but the first certain date we have for him is April 1822, when he married a Kingston girl, Hannah, daughter of Harvey and Catharine Burnett Roode, for whom he named the house which he built later in life (1847) on Union Street. Counter was a baker by trade and followed that trade successfully while he extended his commercial interests. Within a few years he was investing in the Cataraqui Bridge Company. In 1836 he formed the Marine Railway Company to build vessels for both lake and ocean service. He built a dock and warehouse, taking advantage of the need for trans-shipment facilities. He was actively interested in all the enterprises that would promote the interests of Kingston: shipping, canals, bridges, railways.

Counter was also a churchman. He belonged to the Wesleyan Methodists, and was a trustee of their Board at the time when the Sydenham Street Church was built.

Most of all, Counter was a devoted public servant. He served three terms as Mayor of the town when Kingston was the capital. In that capacity he went to London, England, to raise funds for the City Hall and later joined with John A. Macdonald to present a clock for the tower. When Kingston became a city in 1846 Counter was chosen as the first Mayor and in recognition the Lord Mayor of London, England, presented him with a mantel-piece. Counter served four more terms as Mayor, resigning in June 1855 because of business failures. He had made a brief excursion into politics in 1854 when he opposed John A. Macdonald, losing 265 to Macdonald's 427.

In 1841, when the Board of Trade called on well-housed Kingstonians to provide homes for government officials, Counter gave up Plymouth Square; Robert Jamieson, a government judicial officer, moved in. After Counter's business failure in 1855 the building was occupied by a number of commercial tenants. Now (1966), after having been occupied for over sixty-five years by George Robertson & Sons, wholesale grocers, the building has been sold and its future is uncertain.

The south end of the building is designed as a separate unit with a classical gable over a cut-stone projection, but the whole range of buildings is tied together by a wide string course.

Demolished 1973.

Commercial Mart

PRINCESS STREET AT ONTARIO (NOW S & R STORE)

Wilson's Buildings

WELLINGTON STREET AT BROCK (NOW VICTORIA & GREY TRUST)

Mowat's Round Corner Building

PRINCESS STREET AT BAGOT (DEMOLISHED 1974)

These three commercial buildings were designed by George Browne, the architect of the City Hall, and were built in Kingston's boom days, 1841–43. They are markedly similar to each other in design and offer striking examples of the effect of renovations in using, abusing and discarding particular architectural features.

The COMMERCIAL MART was originally a house and store built about 1820 and bought in 1837 by Charles Hales, commission merchant. In 1839 Hales moved his family to Bellevue House, his new villa outside the town, and rented the living quarters over the store. In 1841 two more large house-and-store sections were added to the Commercial Mart, continuing the design of ground-floor arches, string course and round-corner construction, an evident favourite with George Browne. An attic storey was added to the whole building with classical pediments to the many dormers.

After many years of commercial use the building became a piano factory, then later was bought by the federal government for warehouse and office space. A disastrous fire in the early 1900s destroyed much of the interior and subsequent renovations have left little, if any, of the original interior. The present owners have made excellent and tasteful use of the ground-floor arches as an arcade.

WILSON'S BUILDINGS, finished by August 1842, were built for William Henry Wilson on the site of his father-in-law's inn. The three-storey and attic construction with four shops on the ground floor and four dwellings above was typical of the period. By 1844 the complete top floor of the block was occupied as a hotel and Wilson had moved to Newcourt, his new country house opposite what is now Lake Ontario Park. The cut-stone work, pilasters and elaborate cornice are those of a fine 1840 building, and in 1972 the ground-floor arches and round corner were restored, Wilfred Sorenson, architect.

MOWAT'S ROUND CORNER BUILDING at Princess and Bagot was built in 1841 as two houses and shops. Its owner was

John Mowat, one of the founders of Queen's University. Mowat, like Hales and Wilson, soon made his home outside the town limits in a double stone house on College Street, but he carried on his grocery business at his Round Corner Building and his second son and partner, George L. Mowat, occupied the living quarters with his family for a few years longer. In 1849 they sold the business, leased the shop and rented the upper part for use as a hotel. Nothing of the original face of the ground floor has survived and few people have ever looked up to see the round corner which was once a landmark.

33

Old Sydenham Ward

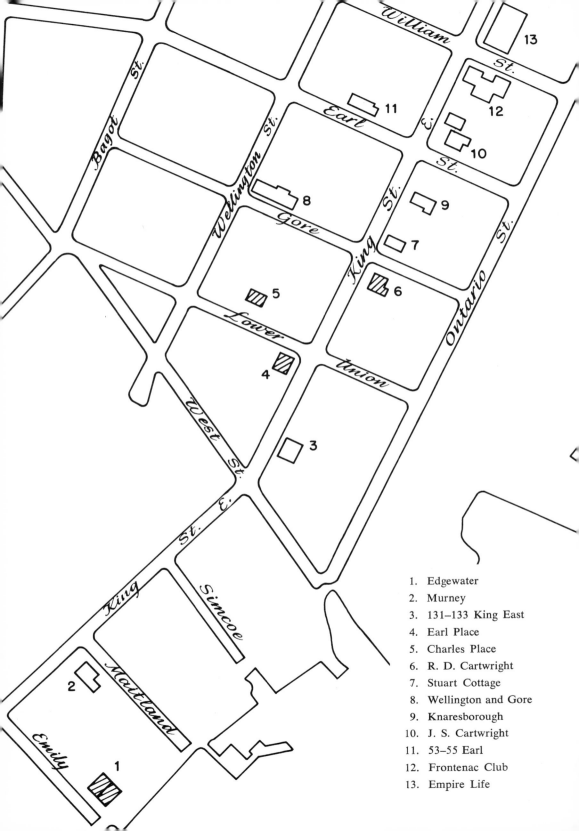

1. Edgewater
2. Murney
3. 131–133 King East
4. Earl Place
5. Charles Place
6. R. D. Cartwright
7. Stuart Cottage
8. Wellington and Gore
9. Knaresborough
10. J. S. Cartwright
11. 53–55 Earl
12. Frontenac Club
13. Empire Life

OLD SYDENHAM WARD

THE PRESENT Sydenham Ward is bounded by William and Barrie streets and the waterfront. The old section of the ward lies between Bagot Street, once called Rear Street, and the waterfront. Wharves and shipyards were established along this section of the shore as the town expanded, and soon commercial houses extended along much of Ontario Street.

King Street, however, only one block inland, was primarily residential. There were two bank buildings at the east corners of William and King—the present Empire Life office, built in 1853 for the Commercial Bank, and the Frontenac Club Apartments, built in 1845 for the Bank of Montreal.

John Solomon Cartwright had his law office in the wing attached to his stone house, built in 1834, at the northeast corner of King and Earl. That same year Mrs. Ann Macaulay built Knaresborough Cottage (now No. 203) in the next block. Archdeacon G. O. Stuart had moved, at the time of his second marriage in 1816, into the cottage at the northeast corner of Gore and King. The cottage, now obscured by later additions and alterations, is said to have been one of those moved from Carleton Island (see p. 7).

On Wellington and Bagot streets and on the cross streets there were modest frame and stone dwellings. During the building boom of 1841–43 the number of houses was doubled as places were built for rent to government officials. Many of the good stone houses in this area were built at that time: cottage rows, double houses and triple houses. The double stone house with arched driveway at 53–55 Earl Street, near King, was built then, and one half of it was rented to army officers. A three-storey triple house was built at the northeast corner of Wellington and Gore—just one of many.

The houses were rented immediately. A big double house on King Street (now Nos. 131–133) was hurriedly finished to house Sir Charles Metcalfe while Sir Charles Bagot lay dying in Alwington House. A local editor wrote that they seemed to be plotting the death of another Governor General by putting him in a house where the plaster was not yet dry.

The town limits had been extended beyond West Street to include Farm

(*continued on page 46*)

Cartwright House

Cartwright House was finished in the spring of 1833 for the Reverend Robert David Cartwright and his bride Harriet Dobbs of Dublin, Ireland.

The Cartwright family has been intimately involved in the life of Kingston and of Canada since this area was first settled. Richard Cartwright, a native of London, England, landed in New York in 1741, and in 1743 married Joanna Beasley of Albany. His sympathies with the Loyalists having been discovered, he and his wife were escorted, under armed guard, to the British lines. Their only son, also named Richard, who was secretary to Colonel Butler of the Queen's Rangers during the Revolutionary War, married Magdalen Secord of Niagara in 1784 and settled near his parents in Kingston about 1787. His forwarding business figures prominently in the history of early commerce in Upper Canada, and he was a member of the Legislative Council. The youngest sons in his family of six boys and two girls were twins: John Solomon, who became a lawyer, banker, judge and member of the Legislative Assembly, and Robert David.

Robert David, a graduate of Queen's College, Oxford, was appointed assistant minister at St. George's in 1831. In 1832, before he left for Ireland and his marriage to Harriet Dobbs, his house was started. Harriet's Letter Book tells of their arrival at Kingston on June 5, 1833, and covers in some detail her first ten years in Canada.

Five children were born to the Reverend Robert David and Mrs. Cartwright. The most famous son, Richard John, later Sir Richard, became Minister of Finance and later Minister of Trade and Commerce in Ottawa, and was for forty years chief spokesman for the Liberal party on fiscal matters.

The house was put up for rent when the Reverend Robert David Cartwright died in May 1843. In 1877 Sheriff William Ferguson bought it, and in 1927 his heirs sold it to the people who now own it, the McLeods.

The white pillared portico and elegant doorway give distinction to this house of simple but well-proportioned lines. The entire façade is of dressed stone blocks, with shadow patterns made by rusticated angle quoins, a plain stone belt marking the floor line, and the stone enframement of the first-floor windows. Outwardly the house is the same as described in a letter of 1833. The stone and iron arrowhead fence is original also. The layout inside is typically eighteenth-century English with upstairs drawing room. The servants' rooms are over the kitchen in a separate wing.

The original stable and coach house have been converted to a garage and modern apartment. Otherwise the house and grounds have been carefully preserved with as little change as possible.

39

Earl Place

This English-style town house was built for Captain Hugh Earl on the site of an earlier frame house belonging to him.

Hugh Earl, as an officer in the Provincial Marine Department, was granted 1,600 acres of land and some town lots in Kingston. Other town lots and Park Lot 2 (the present West, Earl, William and Johnson streets above Bagot) were granted to his wife, Anne Earl, daughter of Molly Brant and Sir William Johnson. Anne was one of six daughters of this remarkable Indian woman. Molly Brant's story includes life on a big estate in the Mohawk Valley as the consort of Sir William Johnson, flight to Canada during the American Revolution, control of troublesome Indians with the British forces in Upper Canada and the gratitude of a government expressed in grants of land and a home to "Miss Molly" and her children. In 1783 Molly Brant's house was built on the shore of the Cataraqui River at the northern edge of Kingston but it disappeared long ago.

Hugh Earl, a native of Ayrshire, Scotland, was commissioned as 2nd Lieutenant and mate in the Marine Department. He was Master of *Moira* when, on March 30, 1812, he succeeded Captain John Steel as senior commander on Lake Ontario and assumed command of *Royal George*. Of the Earls' three daughters only Jane survived her father when he died in

January 1841, in his seventy-seventh year. Jane, wife of Colin Miller, died with no issue, and the lands were inherited by J. B. W. Kerr, a great-grandson of Molly Brant, and sold.

In 1874 Dr. Orlando Strange bought Earl Place and changed the name to Montague Place. Thirty-five years later it became a club house and is now an apartment building.

The house is built of smooth-faced rubble. It has a shallow front projection with a pediment and a further projection holds the doorway. The side façade has four false and two real windows, a not unusual arrangement to keep a balanced design. Inside, the stair sweeps up in a graceful curve.

Charles Place

There is reason to believe that this house was built as early as 1820, certainly before February 1832, when the lot and all the buildings on it were bought by James Nickalls, Jr., husband of Ann Louisa Oliver, from John Blake and wife. (Nothing is now known about the Blakes.) The Oliver family owned Charles Place for sixty-six years.

Nickalls was a lawyer and, as such, a member of the Law Society of Upper Canada. This Society for the establishment of rules and regulations within the profession was organized by fifteen lawyers then practising in Upper Canada, among them Allan McLean of Kingston. The Law Society admitted students, called men to the bar and appointed new Benchers to the Society. By the Provincial Act of 1822 the Society was incorporated and its regulations were made law. James Nickalls, Jr., who was among the students at law that year, was called to the bar in 1824, and practised law in Kingston.

The Nickalls may have made some changes when they moved into the house, for some of the interior woodwork seems to be of the late 1830s. There was more extensive renovation in the 1840s when Charles Oliver and his wife moved in with Charles's sister, Mrs. Nickalls, then a widow. The attic storey, which had been servants' quarters accessible only by a narrow steep stair, was converted into family bedrooms, the Gothic gable over the door was added and a stair was built in the centre hall. The house was then called Charles Place to distinguish it from a near-by house occupied by George Oliver.

Charles Place is particularly interesting to architects for its umbrage, or recessed verandah, a rare feature in Upper Canada. They remark also the doorway and windows and the quality of design which distinguishes this cottage and which has been preserved with remarkable care.

43

Edgewater

John Hamilton had this handsome double house built for his two married children who lived in Kingston, Clark Hamilton and Isabella Hamilton Paton, and deeded it to them in 1859.

John Hamilton, a brother of Peter Hunter Hamilton after whom Hamilton, Ontario, was named, was the third son of Robert Hamilton by his second wife, Mary Herchmer. Robert Hamilton came to Upper Canada from New York during the American Revolution and was a partner of Richard Cartwright, first at Carleton Island and later at Queenston and Kingston.

John, educated in Edinburgh, returned to Canada in 1818 and entered his father's forwarding business, taking charge of the Kingston office. His many Herchmer cousins made him welcome and the family bonds were strengthened in 1829 when he married Frances Macpherson, whose brother John was Jane Herchmer's husband. In 1831 John Hamilton became a member of the Legislative Council, a position he held until his death in 1882. He was President of the Commercial Bank of Kingston and for forty-two years was on the Board of Trustees of Queen's University. When Kingston became the capital of Canada he bought from Mrs. Henry Murney part of this block on the waterfront and built his own house (now demolished) there in 1841.

Emily Street, where Edgewater stands, was once the subject of a court case involving Mayor Thomas Kirkpatrick and two members of the Board of Health. The charge was "obstructing a street, Emily, by building a hospital; and harbouring diseased persons in the park." This was during a cholera epidemic in 1847 when Irish immigrants, fleeing the potato famine, were sickening and dying from Grosse Ile to the farthest reaches of Upper Canada. The three men were convicted but never sentenced, and the temporary hospital was moved from Emily Street.

Edgewater has a beautiful site on the water's edge, facing a park, to enhance its skilfully designed nineteenth-century architecture. The two doors, round-arched, stand together in a single projection and are flanked by bay windows. Above the wide eaves of the hipped roof are dormers which are obviously later, non-matching additions.

44

45

(*continued from page 37*)

Lot 25—the present City Park and waterfront area. When the government bought the park area as a site for the proposed Parliament Building, **the** Murneys, who had bought Farm Lot 25 from Michael Grass, were suddenly in a position to make a large amount of money. They sold lots on the south side of King Street to a select few and big houses were built. Mrs. **Murney** built the pleasant stone house at the southwest corner of King and Maitland streets.

Then suddenly the boom was over. Perhaps this sudden break in the real estate market and the slow recovery saved old Sydenham Ward. Buildings which might have been torn down in the name of progress, to the loss of us all, are still standing.

46

The First Subdivisions

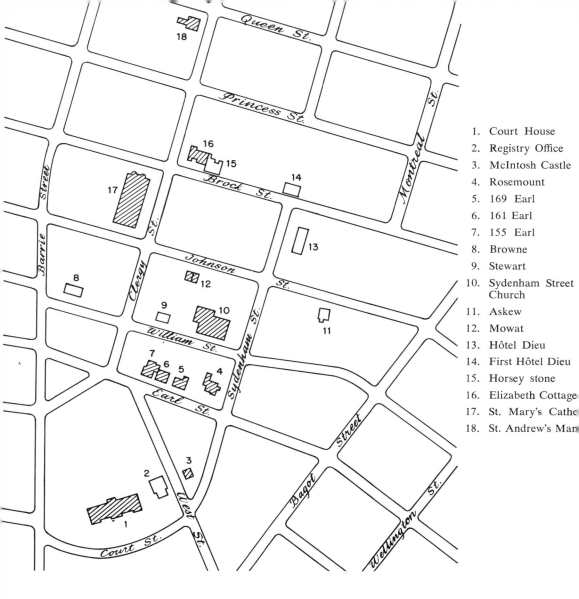

1. Court House
2. Registry Office
3. McIntosh Castle
4. Rosemount
5. 169 Earl
6. 161 Earl
7. 155 Earl
8. Browne
9. Stewart
10. Sydenham Street Church
11. Askew
12. Mowat
13. Hôtel Dieu
14. First Hôtel Dieu
15. Horsey stone
16. Elizabeth Cottage
17. St. Mary's Cathe
18. St. Andrew's Man

THE FIRST SUBDIVISIONS

MOST OF THIS AREA was outside the original townsite. Park Lot 1 included both sides of Brock Street and the north side of Johnson Street from Bagot to Barrie. The Crown grant to Sir John Johnson was sold to the Reverend Father Alexander Macdonell, who named it Selma Park and subdivided it.

48

Park Lot 2, granted to Anne Earl, included the area from Johnson Street to West Street between Bagot and Clergy. It was subdivided and sold in the 1840s. A triangular section in the Barrie, Clergy, William streets area was part of Farm Lot 25, a Crown grant to Michael Grass, bought by Henry Murney and sold by his widow.

Selma Park was the first section to be subdivided. It was there, in 1838, that Regiopolis College, now the central section of Hôtel Dieu Hospital, was started. Soon lots on Brock Street were sold and stone houses built. In 1843 John A. Macdonald and his bride moved into an elegant house near the corner of Brock and Barrie streets; it was burned in 1856. On Brock Street at the end of Sydenham the Sisters of the Religious Hospitallers of St. Joseph bought a big stone house for a hospital and in September 1845 the first patients were being cared for. For forty-six years the Sisters ministered to the sick in that building until they bought the old Regiopolis College building on Sydenham Street in 1891 and named it the Hôtel Dieu.

In Park Lot 2 a few houses had been built close to Bagot Street along Earl and Johnson streets before the lot was subdivided. Thomas Askew had a double house on Johnson Street, the present 178–180, half of which he rented to John A. Macdonald in the fall of 1849. Mayor John Counter bought a large section of the lot, subdivided it and sold lots along Earl and William streets. James Stewart, architect and contractor, built an elaborate brick mansion on William Street, the present 185.

Charles Hales, merchant, bought the triangular part of Farm Lot 25 in 1841 and subsequently granted lots in this section to James Milner, contractor, and George Browne, architect, as payment for their work on his Commercial Mart Building. Browne built a big house for himself on William Street which Queen's College occupied from 1844 to 1854; after that Queen's Preparatory School took over and still later the house was a residence for women students of Queen's. Today it is an apartment building.

As Kingston grew, the first subdivisions were built up slowly with churches, schools and the solid, substantial homes of the merchant and professional classes. Many of the original homes are still standing, most of them now converted into apartments.

St. Mary's Roman Catholic Cathedral

Tenders were called in June 1843 for St. Mary's Cathedral, and five years later, in October 1848, it was consecrated. For forty years Roman Catholics had worshipped at St. Joseph's, generally called "the French Church," built in 1808 at the northeast corner of Bagot and William streets (now demolished).

The arrival of the Reverend Father (later Bishop) Alexander Macdonell in 1803 marked the beginning of a rapid increase in numbers and property of Roman Catholics in Kingston. The use of St. George's Anglican Church was granted and Father Macdonell celebrated mass there until St. Joseph's was built. He had the whole province from Lake Superior to the Quebec border under his care for about ten years and he laid the foundation of his church in Upper Canada, going by canoe, on horseback and sometimes on foot. Before his death, which took place in 1840, churches, chapels, schools and other institutions had been established in forty-eight parishes or missions in Ontario. In 1838 Bishop Macdonell laid the cornerstone of Regiopolis College, now part of Hôtel Dieu Hospital. Bonnycastle wrote that at the ceremony the Bishop, then seventy-nine, was "supported on his right and left by the arms of a Presbyterian colonel and a colonel of the Church of England."

The Reverend Father Réni Gaulin was Bishop when the cornerstone of St. Mary's Roman Catholic Cathedral was laid—then in the fields at the edge of the town. It was made of stone quarried on the spot, an impressive building 210 feet long by 88 feet wide, built in the Gothic style with massive pillars. Between 1885 and 1890 a new front and the present 200-foot tower were built; stained-glass windows were installed and the seating capacity was increased. To celebrate the elevation of the Diocese to an Archiepiscopal See, the Chapel of St. James of Boanarges was built at the rear of the Cathedral. The architect for the improvements and the Chapel was J. Connolly of Toronto; the contractor, William Newlands of Kingston.

After 1898 further improvements were made to the interior, including the installation of an organ. In 1910 the interior was completely redecorated by Panzironi of New York and the main altar was put in its present position. Panzironi's son renewed the decoration in 1958.

The Archbishop's house, on Johnson Street just west of the Cathedral, was built in 1848 after the Cathedral was consecrated.

Mowat Houses

This double limestone house was built in 1852 for John Mowat after he had retired from the grocery business that he and his second son, George, had carried on in the Round Corner Building on Princess Street.

George, then twenty-seven and married, entered Queen's College, where he won all the prizes in mathematics. After two years he left to read law and later became the partner of Alexander Campbell. George and his family lived in one of the Mowat houses and his parents in the other. John Mowat's eldest son, Oliver, who was to become Premier of Ontario and later Lieutenant-Governor, had moved to Toronto after articling with John A. Macdonald and practising law for a few years in Kingston. The third son, the Reverend John B. Mowat, returned from his charge in Niagara in 1857 to become Professor of Theology at Queen's, and moved in with his parents. For fifty-one years the western house remained in the possession of the family and for eighty-six years the eastern house.

John Mowat, born in Canisby, Scotland, in 1791, enlisted when he was sixteen in the 3rd Buffs. When his regiment was recalled to England from Canada in 1814, he procured his discharge and settled in Kingston. He was an excellent example of a discharged soldier who made a success of his life and contributed greatly to the development of Upper Canada. When he died in 1860 in his sixty-ninth year, he had seen a village grow to a city with ties of trade and commerce throughout the province.

Besides his grocery interests John Mowat was involved in other business ventures: the Commercial Bank, of which he was a director for many years, the Kingston Gas Company, the Building Society and the Board of Trade. He was one of the first to be appointed an elder of St. Andrew's Presbyterian Church in 1822, and was a devoted worker for the church all his life. He was deeply interested in education and used both his money and his influence to make a better education available to Upper Canadians—especially Presbyterians. He was one of the fourteen men who met at St. Andrew's Church to establish a college in Kingston, and he served long and faithfully on the property committee, whose duty it was to find, keep in repair and pay for accommodation for the struggling college.

The Mowat Houses, with their dressed stone fronts and rubble stone sides, are most interesting for the paired windows and stone window balconies. The mansard roof was an addition, probably in the late 1860s.

Elizabeth Cottage

The eastern section of the present Elizabeth Cottage was built by Edward Horsey about 1841–43. He was born in Devonshire, trained with a builder in London and came to Kingston in 1832. Horsey was first listed as a carpenter; then he advertised as a master builder; and, after some success, he called himself architect, as was then the custom. He returned to England in 1840, evidently planning to settle there, for he sold his library of builders' manuals.

A year later he was back in Kingston to stay. The building of the original Elizabeth Cottage followed two successful housing ventures for rental purposes—one the double stone building beside the Cottage, the other a row of brick houses for eighteen tenants on Clergy Street between Brock and Princess, no longer standing. In 1848 Horsey succeeded William Coverdale as architect of the Provincial Penitentiary and in 1855 was the architect of the Frontenac County Court House.

Elizabeth Cottage, Regency Gothic in style, a bit of romantic whimsy, is said to be reminiscent of Horsey's family home in Sherborne, Dorset, England. The false gable, the open tracery of the sham buttresses, verge boards, pinnacles and oriole window are in sharp contrast to the big, three-storey, double terrace building beside the Cottage. The original Cottage was joined by a high stone wall to a carriagehouse and stable on the west, which was later demolished to make way for a smaller house carefully adapted to the style of the original Cottage. The joining of the two to make the present Elizabeth Cottage has been accomplished with skill, although the sunroom added to the eastern section somewhat spoils the design. The interior is delightfully designed and in excellent condition.

Edward Horsey's daughter Elizabeth and her husband, Dr. Fyfe Fowler, were the second occupants of the Cottage. They had four daughters and a son, none of whom married. Miss Louisa was the third mistress of the Cottage, and she and her surviving sister, Catherine, decided that it should become a residence for elderly ladies obliged to give up their homes. Accordingly, in 1955 Elizabeth Cottage was opened as a home for retired gentlewomen as stipulated in the will of Edward Horsey's grand-daughter, Miss Louisa Fowler. The furniture and furnishings of the Fowlers have been left for the use of the residents. Meals are served at a walnut table set with cutlery bearing the Horsey family crest.

St. Andrew's Manse

The Manse was built in 1841–42 to a design by George Browne, architect, and sits beside St. Andrew's Presbyterian Church.

The first church on that site was built in 1820 with funds raised by the Presbyterian Society of Kingston. Before that, the adherents of the Church of Scotland in Kingston had been served by ministers from surrounding communities, including the Reverend John Bethune of Williamstown, the Reverend Robert McDowall of Sandhurst and the Reverend William Bell of Perth. The Reverend John Barclay of Kettle, Scotland, who was inducted in 1820 when the first church building was finished, became the first minister of the Scotch Presbyterian Church in Kingston.

During Dr. Barclay's ministry there was a heated controversy over the claim made by the Reverend George O. Stuart of St. George's Church that the Church of England had the sole rights of baptism, marriage and burial. In the settlement of the dispute the rights of the Church of Scotland were recognized but not before appeal had had to be made to the Lieutenant-Governor of Upper Canada.

In 1827 the Reverend John Machar became the second minister of St. Andrew's and served a large congregation for thirty-seven years. Dr. Machar worked closely with Archdeacon Stuart and the Reverend Robert Cartwright of St. George's in establishing free schools in the district. He was also an organizer of the group that met in St. Andrew's to consider the establishment of a college to train ministers for the Church of Scotland— a college which was to become Queen's University.

Until 1841 the ministers of St. Andrew's had lived in rented houses; prosperity made a proper manse possible. George Browne's original, beautiful Regency design has been carefully preserved. The rough ashlar of the walls is contrasted by the cut-stone surrounds to the windows and doors and a cut-stone string course. The large windows have the original sash with the narrow outer panes characteristic of this period. The chimneys are grouped to form a single central stack on the roof. The wooden side verandah on the east is balanced by the kitchen wing and a stone wall on the west. St. Andrew's Manse is a building of quality.

Frontenac County Court House

The Court House is a symbol of the development of district government in Canada. The building of the first Court House, which stood at the corner of King and Clarence streets on the site of the present Customs House, was authorized in 1796 by the Magistrates of the Court of Quarter Sessions of the Midland District, who were appointed in 1788 in the transfer of authority from military to civil government. Early courts had been held in inns alternately in Kingston and Adolphustown, but after the 1796 Court House was built the superior courts sat only in Kingston.

With the growing population of the area and the increased complication of the law the old Court House and Gaol were too small long before 1853 when the County Council advertised them for sale. Contracts were let in July 1855 for the erection of this second Court House and Gaol on land obtained from the provincial government. The buildings were to serve the united counties of Frontenac, Lennox and Addington. Edward Horsey was the architect; Scobell and Tossell were the contractors. The cost was £20,000. The first session of court was held in the new building in November 1858 and construction had then been started on the new Gaol and residence for the gaoler immediately behind the new Court House.

In 1874 the building was gutted by fire and rebuilt on the original plans with George Newlands as the contractor. At that time the County Registry Office was built just to the east to relieve the crowded condition of the Court House. In 1931 another fire damaged one of the wings. The interior has been almost completely rebuilt (1965–66) to improve the accommodation for court and county officials. In this renovation the entrances at each end of the building have been changed and glass panels have been put in the huge front doors, but otherwise the façade has been carefully preserved.

The standard classical elements seen in the City Hall are used in the Court House on a smaller, finer scale. The wings are shorter than those in the City Hall and have gables in front. Although the height to the top of the dome is only 80 feet the building seems much taller because of its site on a small rise and the upward thrust of the six massive pillars of the portico. Most of the stone was quarried on the site but the stone for the pillars was brought from Chaumont Bay in the state of New York.

McIntosh Castle

The Castle is said, by a descendant of John Power, its architect, to have been the first building he designed when he started business for himself about 1849. Power, a Devonshire man and son of an English architect, came to Kingston in 1846 and worked for a time with Edward Horsey, architect. Power designed a number of Kingston churches and commercial buildings but the Castle is unique. It seems likely that the design was dictated by Power's client, Donald McIntosh of Glasgow, who promised his family a castle.

McIntosh had a general shipping agency in 1849, conducting a branch of the Quebec Forwarding Company, and receiving, storing and shipping property of every description. Later he was the owner of the steamship *Inkerman*—one of the forty steamers, thirty-five schooners, three brigantines, barges and other craft owned in and operated from Kingston in the middle 1850s. Because there was little manufacturing in Upper Canada the imports of finished goods and the exports of raw material kept shipping for a considerable time the most important business. But as methods of transportation became diversified the shipping trade could be seen to have overexpanded. The transportation of small cargoes had shifted to the railroads, and when the crops failed, a recession in shipping set in which vitally affected Kingston.

McIntosh had financial difficulties and, so the story goes, had to leave his Castle before it was completed. Joseph Doyle, shipbroker and insurance agent, bought and finished the house. For many years the Reverend James Brock lived there and the house is still privately owned.

The octagonal tower topped by battlements and the design of the wings with small gables, verge boards and finials contribute to the feeling of whimsy—a small castle of someone's dreams. The front door and entrance steps have been changed. The Castle is particularly fortunate in its setting on a high corner overlooking City Park.

Rosemount

Earl Street houses, 155-169

These limestone houses can be considered as a group for they were all built between 1847 and 1850. Earl Street, above Bagot, was part of Park Lot 2 granted to Anne Earl and was outside the original town line. It became one of the early subdivisions to be included in the city.

This was a period of expansion in Kingston as in all Upper Canada. Settlements were pushing back the frontiers and lake ports were expanding to meet the demands for goods. Merchants were prospering and people could afford and demand the creature comforts being established in settled areas: waterworks, gasworks, better fire protection and better schools.

ROSEMOUNT was built for Edward H. Hardy, a dry goods merchant, in 1849–50. His daughter, Grace, Mrs. Edgerton Rees, lived there after his death. It is now an apartment house.

The house is a Tuscan villa somewhat similar to Bellevue House but much heavier and less gay. The tall ornamented chimneys and fine iron fence remain, but large plate-glass windows replace the fine early ones.

NO. 155 was built by Samuel Shaw, a merchant, in 1848–49 and sold in 1854 to John Kerr, manager of the gasworks. A rather plain house with good chimneys, the original sash contributes to its architectural quality.

NO. 161 was started in 1847 and not quite finished when John Fraser and his bride, Catharine, daughter of John Mowat, moved there in September 1848. He was a wholesale hardware merchant. The Frasers had ten children and also brought from Scotland some of their nephews to attend Queen's University.

NO. 169, now called Machar House, was built for William Grant about 1849–50. John Breden bought it for his daughter, Mrs. Henry Cunningham, about 1870. Somewhat later fire destroyed the upper storey but it was rebuilt. In 1932 it was opened as the Agnes Maule Machar Home for Protestant Women, named in honour of the Reverend J. M. Machar's only daughter.

There is a similarity in these three homes: proportioned façade, arched door opening, two transomed windows on the main floor balanced by three windows above. Each has a string course and is bracketed, No. 169 being the plainest. The porches differ: the one on No. 155 is believed to be original, but the other two are additions of different dates.

155 EARL STREET

161 EARL STREET

169 EARL STREET

Sydenham Street United Church

This church was built in 1851–52 to serve the Wesleyan Methodists, who had been using the old Union Church on the site of the present Masonic Temple at Wellington and Johnson streets.

William Coverdale, the architect chosen for the new building, came from Quebec in 1832 to build the Penitentiary for the provincial government in the village of Portsmouth, on the western outskirts of Kingston. He served as City Architect, as architect for the Lunatic Asylum (now Ontario Hospital) and designed many of the big houses and commercial buildings in Kingston. The Board of Wesleyan Methodists—Mayor John Counter, chairman—admired Coverdale's design for St. James Anglican Church (1845–47) and hired him as architect for their new church.

Among the Methodists in Kingston, as elsewhere in Upper Canada, there were Methodist Episcopals from the United States, British Wesleyans, Primitive Methodists, American Methodists and others. One result of this grouping and regrouping was the widespread and protracted controversy over the ownership of Methodist churches.

Kingston had two early Methodist chapels; the Reverend Joseph Stinson and the Reverend Egerton Ryerson preached in them in the 1835–36 period. Following the opening of Sydenham Street Church in 1852, the Bay Street Chapel group met in Ontario Hall in the City Hall until 1864, when they built the first Queen Street Methodist Church. Another group in Williamsville, a suburb at about the present Victoria Street area on Princess Street, moved from their early chapel to the Princess Street Church about 1885.

Sydenham Street Church has had many improvements and enlargements since it was built in 1852. The tower and spire were added in 1854. Some time later, a church hall was built. In 1962–63 the hall was greatly enlarged and a small chapel was also built.

Farm Lot 24

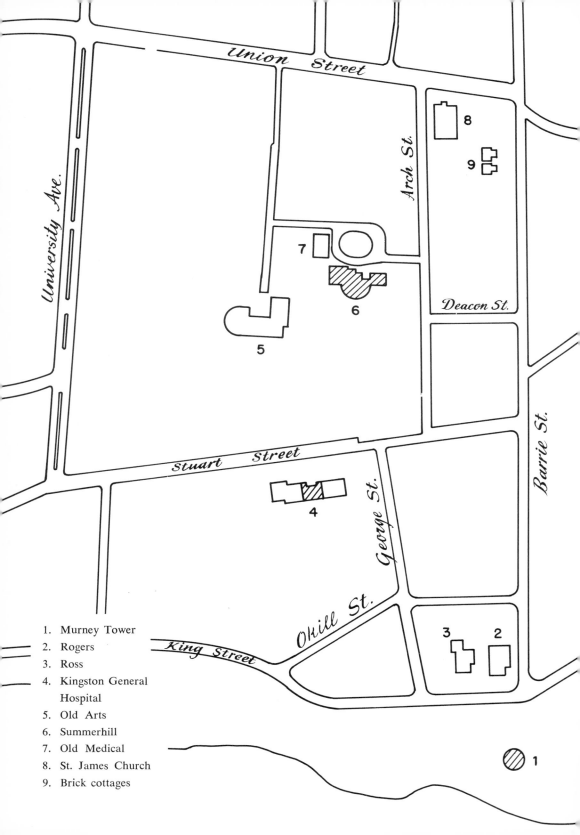

Union Street

University Ave.

Arch St.

8

9

7

6

5

Deacon St.

Barrie St.

Stuart Street

4

George St.

Okill St.

King Street

3

2

1. Murney Tower
2. Rogers
3. Ross
4. Kingston General
   Hospital
5. Old Arts
6. Summerhill
7. Old Medical
8. St. James Church
9. Brick cottages

1

FARM LOT 24

FARM LOT 24 included the land from Barrie Street to University Avenue and from the waterfront north to Concession Street. The Reverend Dr. John Stuart, who had received the Crown grant of the lot as a Loyalist and as the former Chaplain of Sir John Johnson's Regiment, farmed the land to support his family. His son and heir, Archdeacon G. O. Stuart, taking advantage of a rising real estate market in 1838, subdivided part of the lot and sold building sites. The most desirable of these were on the lakeshore and on Barrie Street, but clusters of small cottages were built north of Union Street and near Princess Street.

Here, as in other areas outside the original townsite, a small village grew up—its nucleus a wayside inn. The organization of Stuartville, as the village was called, was encouraged and supported by all the householders on Lot 24. Their common purpose was to oppose annexation by Kingston, for they objected to being saddled with the debt which Kingston had incurred to build the City Hall. They fought annexation with vigour and often with vituperation. But in 1850 the argument was settled against them by the Municipal Act, which had a special section providing for the annexation of Farm Lot 24 and other lands to the city of Kingston.

Not many of the early houses are left. Thomas Rogers, an architect, built himself a modest house at the corner of Barrie and King about 1830. It was enlarged in 1865 and again in 1905, the portico being part of this second addition. Next door on King Street, Charles Ross, a bank manager, built a mansion of yellow brick in 1859. It is now a nurses' residence.

The poet, Charles Sangster, lived in one of the twin brick cottages on Barrie Street near Union. The site for St. James Anglican Church, round the corner on Union, was given by the Honourable John Macaulay. William Coverdale was the architect and the church was built in 1845.

Five streets near the Kingston General Hospital honour the subdivider of Farm Lot 24: Arch, Deacon, George, Okill and Stuart.

Murney Tower

Murney Tower is one of the four martello towers built in Kingston in the 1846–48 period. They were originally planned by the British Royal Engineers in 1829 as part of an elaborate system of defence to protect Kingston from the Americans.

Experience in the War of 1812 had shown that Kingston needed greater protection, and in the meantime it had gained in significance as a port and military centre and as the southern terminal for the Rideau Canal system. By 1836 Fort Henry (the new one) was almost complete but the system of defensive works planned to encircle Kingston was delayed. Later the sudden spurt of growth and increase in land values connected with the choice of Kingston as capital made the plans obsolete and impractical. With the Oregon Crisis in 1845 some immediate action became imperative, however, and the towers, which could be erected quickly, were started. Before they were finished the Oregon Treaty was signed.

Murney Tower was occupied by the militia at one time and later was used for a while as the home of some militia families. By 1890 it had become obsolete and was abandoned. In 1925 the Kingston Historical Society opened it as a museum and it is now open to the public every summer.

The interior of the building is a true circle but the outside is not, because, in order to give greater protection against ships on the lake, the thickness of the wall was varied from 8 feet at the base on the north side to 15 on the south. Earthwork surrounds a dry moat which is protected by small loop-holed chambers extending from the walls.

The arch forming the ceiling of the main floor is remarkable stonework. A winding stair in the stone wall leads to the gun platform on top, now protected by a wooden roof. The thirty-two pounder cannon is mounted on a circular track so that it can be swung to any point.

Below the main floor are a number of rooms, including a powder magazine, lined with special brickwork. There are no nails in the floor because of the danger of striking a spark that would set off the gunpowder.

Another feature of the tower is the system for supplying water in time of siege: rain water was collected in a cistern, and even the cooking steam was condensed in the heavy iron cauldrons on the fire box.

Kingston General Hospital

STUART STREET

In September 1831 a citizens' committee met to plan a drive to raise £1,000 toward the erection of a hospital in Kingston. A list dated 1832, which gives the names of the subscribers, bears annotations—"dead," or "left town"—which were added at a later date, presumably in the course of the campaign. The Provincial Parliament made a grant of £3,000 and the hospital was started in 1833. Thomas Rogers was superintending architect, using plans from Wells and Thompson of Montreal.

By June 1835, the building itself—a fine structure, three storeys high, 89 feet 4 inches long, 53 feet 4 inches wide —was complete. It had two fronts, approached by handsome flights of stone steps. The south front was then the main entrance.

But there were no furnishings or equipment, and the funds were exhausted. For three years the building was empty; then during the Rebellion of 1837–38 it was used as barracks for the military.

When Kingston was made the capital of Canada in 1841 the hospital became the Parliament Building. George Browne, architect, was hired to make some necessary changes: moving partitions and installing seats to be ready for the first sitting of the new Parliament on June 14, 1841. In the few years that Parliament met in the hospital, legislation was passed that laid the framework for much of our government. The last sitting there was in November 1843; the government moved to Montreal in 1844.

Once again the hospital building was empty and this time the town was suffering a severe financial depression. By the fall of 1845 the ladies of the Female Benevolent Society had raised enough money to equip two wards which were open to those of the sick who were certified proper recipients of public charity: in those days the ones who could pay were treated at home; only the poor were hospitalized. In 1849 Kingston Hospital was incorporated and came under municipal control. Seven years later the administration was reorganized under a board of governors as it is today.

The first expansion came in 1862 when the Watkins Wing was built to provide care for those with infectious diseases. In the 1880s central heating and gas lighting were installed and some repairs and improvements made. A training course for nurses was established in 1886 and two students were enrolled.

Beginning with the erection of the Nickle Wing in 1890–91 there have been additions and improvements to the hospital every ten years or oftener. The Kingston Hospital that in 1845 was open to a few charity patients, and in 1858 was equipped for only 50 patients, in 1966 has 600 beds.

Kingston Hospital.

[Incorporated by Act of Parliament—144 Beds.]

Admit Mr *Alfred Sales Oliver*
During the hours of Medical attendance.

PERPETUAL.

Jas. Sampson
Prest. Board Governors K.H.

James Hopkirk
Secretary.

Kingston 1st Novr. 1857

Summerhill

Summerhill was built in 1836–39 for Archdeacon George Okill Stuart himself on the finest site on his inheritance. He sold lots along the edge of the farm lot to help pay for the big house, and in 1839 a sale of twenty-five acres to the government at a price of £4,000 allowed him to complete the second wing. Mrs. Stuart was not happy in Summerhill: the stream running through the basement made the house damp; their little cottage in Kingston was far cosier. She was therefore pleased to move back to town when Kingston became the capital and the Archdeacon leased Summerhill to a Mr. Botsford for a boarding house for government officials. The next year the government took it over to provide office space near the Parliament Building.

The Archdeacon's big house was referred to as Stuart's Folly, or the Archdeacon's Great Castle. But in advertising it for rent in 1843 Stuart described it as "a spacious house on Summerhill." No one could afford to rent it, though, and the Stuarts moved back in for a few years.

In July 1853 they began negotiations with the trustees of Queen's to sell the house and grounds to the College. Queen's, by that time, had been in three different houses. The present No. 67 on Colborne Street was used for the first session. Then quarters were rented from a Mr. Weeks on Princess Street, now 320–322, opposite St. Andrew's Church. In 1844, Queen's leased the house on William Street which George Browne, the architect, had built for himself; from there they moved to Summerhill in 1854.

Until 1858, when Old Medical was built, Summerhill housed the entire university: administration, classes, laboratories, library; and it even provided accommodation for a few students. The medical faculty had rooms in the east wing.

In 1867 the centre section became the Principal's residence, and three years later, after the Old Arts Building was finished, the wings were enlarged to become residences for two professors. The Principal and the Vice-Chancellor now occupy the residences in the wings.

Summerhill, one of the great Canadian houses of its time, has had many alterations. On the central block there were originally two quarter-circle porticos and a central porch with three set of stairs. The centre front bay contained the original drawing room and immediately above it the principal bedroom. An elaborate parapet hid the roof. The wings, one storey high, were fronted by colonnades and culminated in blocks two storeys high.

SUMMERHILL 1868

The Shore Road

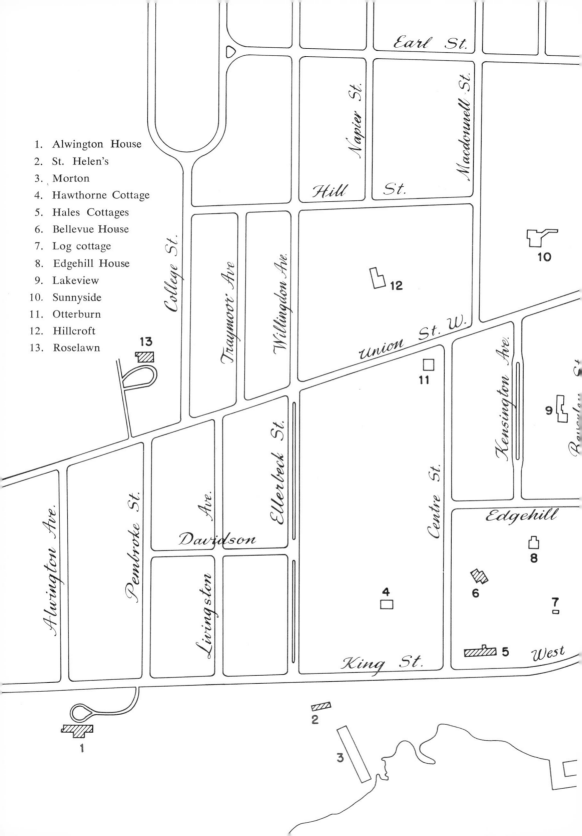

1. Alwington House
2. St. Helen's
3. Morton
4. Hawthorne Cottage
5. Hales Cottages
6. Bellevue House
7. Log cottage
8. Edgehill House
9. Lakeview
10. Sunnyside
11. Otterburn
12. Hillcroft
13. Roselawn

THE SHORE ROAD

A FEW MODEST FARM HOUSES were the first buildings in this area and at least one log cottage, neatly stuccoed, still stands. Then breweries and distilleries were built on the waterfront. In 1831 Thomas Dalton sold his brewery to Thomas Molson, who later sold to James Morton. Morton also took over the operation of Robert Drummond's brewery and distillery (in 1834) and expanded it. Some of Morton's buildings are now used as part of Eastern Ontario Military Headquarters.

The area is most notable for the country estates built between 1834 and 1854. Some bankers, lawyers and merchants had homes there before Kingston became the capital. During the capital boom, good lots were snapped up, often in private deals. The new Queen's College auctioned lots it had acquired in the present College Street area.

About 1836 Francis Harper, a banker, built a big stone house which he called Hawthorne Cottage. In 1841 he rented it to Lord Sydenham's Civil Secretary and George Browne supervised some alterations in it. The original house is now lost in the additions and alterations of the building which houses St. Mary's of the Lake Hospital for Chronic Invalids.

In 1847 Mayor John Counter moved into Otterburn, at the southwest corner of Centre and Union streets, during the building of his new house on Union Street near Macdonell. The house, South Roode Cottage, is now a children's home called Sunnyside. Lakeview, on Beverley Street below Union, was built in 1850 by an architect, John Crawford. It is one of the few houses which has retained its adjacent outbuildings and extensive grounds.

F. M. Hill, a lawyer, commissioned William Coverdale, architect, to build Hillcroft on Union Street; it was not quite finished when Hill died in 1854. For some years it housed a boys' school but it is now a private home. The grounds, which once covered a whole block, have been sold until only a small circle separates Hillcroft from rows of modern dwellings.

Edgehill House was built by 1835 but has been greatly altered. It sits in comparative solitude, hidden by huge trees, in the middle of the block between Beverley and Centre streets. There are two modern houses on King Street where the drive once curved through the trees up to the big house on the hill.

Hales Cottages

This row of stone houses behind walled gardens was built in 1841 by Charles Hales, commission merchant, as rental properties. It is said that a pile of stone for their construction made Lord Sydenham's horse shy and brought about the fall that caused the Governor General's death from gangrene on September 19, 1841.

The desperate need for accommodation for government officials had induced Hales to rent out his new home, Bellevue House, as men of his substance were being asked to do, and he was not slow to realize the strategic position of the land he owned on what was referred to as "the road to the Penitentiary" and later as "the road to Government House." His business instinct proved to be sound: he had no trouble finding tenants for the cottages because they were so conveniently located—half way between the Governor General's residence and the Parliament Building. Even after the capital left Kingston, Hales Cottages were, as they continue to be, valuable properties.

This range of charmingly simple cottages (there were five originally— one was destroyed by fire) is enhanced by the high stone walls and by the horizontal canopy at eaves level which ties the units together. An early advertisement described them as stone cottages of ten rooms well laid out. Recent owners have made additions at the rear and have changed the original dormer fronts. Although the alterations are slight and in good taste, the unity of the row has suffered somewhat. Interiors are in the Greek Revival style popular in the early 1840s.

Bellevue House

35 CENTRE STREET

Bellevue House was built about 1838–40—before his cottages on King Street West—by Charles Hales, commission merchant. From his dwelling over a shop (the Commercial Mart Building) he was moving to a country estate at the same time as other wealthy men were making the same change and were building big houses close by. While Kingston was the capital, however, he, like others, rented his house to government officials and military officers to ease the housing shortage. Afterwards he lived in Bellevue, but only for a short time, moving out in 1845 after the death of his wife.

Hales's most famous tenant in Bellevue House was John A. Macdonald and it is in his honour that the house has become a Historic Site. Macdonald moved his wife and infant son, nurse and servants to Bellevue House late in August 1848. Mrs. Macdonald had just returned to Kingston after three years of illness in the United States. Her doctor advised country air, and since Bellevue was then well out of town and cooled by the lake breezes it seemed an ideal spot. Macdonald referred to the house affectionately as Tea Caddy Castle or Pekoe Pagoda—because of the landlord's business.

The year Macdonald spent in Bellevue was one of sorrow when his son died; of hope when his wife, Isabella, improved in health; and of decision in his political and professional careers. As the member for Kingston he was concerned with the University Bill and its possible effect on Queen's College, with Baldwin's Municipal Bill, which had one section referring specifically to Kingston's boundaries, and with the Rebellion Losses Bill, which was the hottest political issue of the time. During that year Macdonald was involved in the organization of the British American League which, meeting in Kingston, discussed a motion for union of all the provinces.

When John A. Macdonald and family moved back into town, Bellevue stood empty for a time until it was rented to Lieutenant-Colonel Henry P. Wulff of the Royal Engineers, who was there until the spring of 1852.

The William Fergusons and their nine children moved into Bellevue next, and seventeen years later sold it when the family had grown up and moved away. Other owners were Thomas Baker, Colonel P. W. Worsley and James Wilson. John Gilbert, grocer, bought Bellevue in 1907 and his estate sold it fifty-two years later to Dr. J. M. R. Beveridge for his large family. In 1964 the house was bought by the federal government.

In architectural style Bellevue House is Italian Tuscan—a romantic villa. Its heavy limestone walls were stuccoed for a smooth face to emphasize the fretwork eaves, verge boards, balconies and shutters. It is built on an L-shaped plan with square tower in the

middle; and the service and servants'
wing is half a storey lower than the
rest of the house. The interior is in the
original Greek Revival style and has
seventeen rooms varying in size from
a large double drawing room to a tiny
linen room.

Bellevue House was opened to the
public in 1967.

Roselawn

UNION STREET WEST AT COLLEGE

In 1841 David John Smith, a lawyer and son of Peter Smith, a pioneer merchant, bought three lots from Queen's College and built this elegant country home. It was a fashionable area, north of the Governor General's residence and near where the College had a site. A few years later, falling land values, foreclosures and builders' demands for payment caught rich and poor alike, and Smith had to mortgage Roselawn to meet his debts.

When he died in 1848 his executors put the big house up for auction but the sale was not closed until 1851, when it was bought by Henry Smith, Jr., son of the Henry Smith who was dismissed from his post as Warden of the Penitentiary. Henry Smith, Jr., a lawyer and member of Parliament, became Solicitor General, then Speaker of the House and in 1860 was knighted. In 1888 the Smith heirs sold Roselawn and it remained in private hands for many years.

From 1948 to 1969 it was the official residence of the Commandant of the National Defence College, and senior officers from the services of Canada and her allies were entertained in its gracious rooms. Big trees and a wide expanse of green lawn still surround Roselawn. A long high stone wall extends from the west side of the house to an archway that gives access to the yard where stone outbuildings stand.

A wide verandah which ran across the front of the house until about 1960 has been replaced by a smaller portico and a screened area at the east side. The classical doorway opens into a wide hall, and fine stairs are lit by a large Venetian window. Roselawn has retained its elegance both inside and out.

Queen's University purchased the property and maintaining the house, has, in 1974, added a conference hall and low-profile residence buildings to the northeast to create the Donald Gordon Centre for Continuing Education.

St. Helen's

St. Helen's was built in 1837–38 by Thomas Kirkpatrick on twelve acres he bought from Christopher Hagerman. This was a period when those who could afford it were building big houses and moving their families from the upper floors of their business premises in town.

Thomas Kirkpatrick had come from Coolmine, Ireland, about 1820 to live with his sister and her husband, Colonel and Mrs. Colley Lyons Lucas Foster. When Kirkpatrick was admitted to the bar in 1824, he entered the law office of Christopher Hagerman in Kingston. In 1829 he married Helen, second daughter of Judge Alexander Fisher of Adolphustown. They had nine children, the most famous being Sir George Airey Kirkpatrick, Lieutenant-Governor of Ontario.

Thomas Kirkpatrick was the first mayor of Kingston when it was incorporated as a town in the spring of 1838. This was the year he moved into his new house, which was then outside the town limits. A question arose about his eligibility to be Mayor and he resigned, but he was elected to the office again in 1847 when Kingston became a city. In the early 1850s he built a house, Closeburn, next to Edgewater on Emily Street and sold St. Helen's to James Morton, who was operating a brewery and distillery beside it.

Mortonwood, as the Morton family called the house, was selected as the overnight residence for the Prince of Wales, Albert Edward (later King Edward VII), when he was to visit Kingston in 1860. But because of the famous Orange Arch incident the Prince did not come ashore at Kingston.

The Morton executors sold the estate to R. W. Barrow, and in 1907 Edward J. B. Pense, owner and publisher of the *British Whig*, bought the house and gave it another name, Ongwanada, meaning home, sweet home.

During the First World War, when space for military hospitals was desperately needed, the federal government leased the property, and in 1919 bought it outright for use as a Military Headquarters. The name has been changed back to St. Helen's and though necessary additions have been made to the property the outward elegance of the main house has been preserved.

Alwington House

Alwington, burned in 1958 and demolished in 1959, is included here because it was perhaps the most important single dwelling in Kingston and because its story belongs not to Kingston alone but to Canada. During the years 1841 to 1844 Alwington was Government House, the official residence of His Excellency the Governor General of Canada. Much of the basic structure of Canadian government was mapped out there in conversations on the cerise and white figured satin of the rosewood sofa in the state drawing room, or over the carved rosewood table in the Governor General's office. Addresses were presented there, political careers were made and lost. And it was in Alwington House that two of Canada's Governors General died.

Charles William Grant, who built Alwington House, was the son of David Alexander Grant of the 84th Regiment and Marie LeMoyne Grant, fourth Baroness of Longueuil. When the house was finished—in 1834—he brought his wife, Caroline Coffin Grant, and two children, Charles and Charlotte, from Montreal to take up residence.

When the bill for the union of Upper and Lower Canada was passed in the summer of 1840 there were rumours that Kingston might be the site of the capital. Lord Sydenham had reached a decision by September but he made no official announcement until February 6,

1841. Meanwhile negotiations had been under way for accommodation in Kingston, and the lease for Alwington House was signed on February 13, 1841.

George Browne, architect, was brought from Montreal to supervise the alterations and extensions to various buildings. Alwington House, which was built of stone, had a central, two-storey block with symmetrical one-storey wings at each side. To make it a proper Government House a new frame wing, two storeys high, was added to the west side. This new wing contained all the official rooms except the Governor General's office, which was in the old house. Alwington House itself was his private residence and could be kept that way by closing the one door connecting it with the new wing.

Lord Sydenham arrived at Alwington House on May 28, 1841, and on June 15 opened the first Parliament in the building that is now Kingston General Hospital. His major concern was to accomplish in fact the union which had been declared by law. In a remarkably short time he achieved results in administration, law and politics which laid a basis for government but which did little to solve the problems of provincial and imperial relations. He died in Alwington House on September 19, 1841, as a result of a fall from his horse, and it was from Alwington that the funeral procession left for the burial in St. George's Church.

92

Sir Charles Bagot, the new Governor General, arrived in Kingston in January 1842 and his wife and daughters joined him in the summer. Bagot was advised and badgered by both the opposing factions in his government and found that the constitutional and political problems could only be solved by strong leadership. He was not well when he engineered the formation of the Baldwin-Lafontaine Government, and by November he asked permission to resign. He was too ill to move when his successor, Metcalfe, was appointed, and he died in Alwington House on May 19, 1843.

Sir Charles Metcalfe moved into the ill-fated Government House on May 25, and into political troubles. Just over a year later, in June 1844, he left Alwington House to go to Montreal, the new capital.

Charles William Grant's family then returned to Alwington House and continued to occupy it until 1902. The sixth Baron, Charles James Irwin Grant, moved in when his father died in 1848 and lived there until 1862, when he moved his family to France. The following year his sister Charlotte and her husband, the Reverend Joseph A. Allen, moved into the house. They had been abroad for a few years and before that their home had been Ardath House on Wolfe Island. Grant Allen, the novelist, was their son; but it was their five daughters who made the lively social life at Alwington House. In 1910 Senator Henry Wartman Richardson bought Alwington; it belonged to his grandsons when it was burned in 1958.

The house was an imposing structure set in magnificent grounds. The picture shows the southern façade of the building, its fluted pillars rising the full height of the centre block. The main entrance was at the north, with a smaller, single-storey portico and a fine door, with fanlight and side lights, opening into a transverse hall. The drawing room was about twenty feet by forty, and had two fireplaces. The dining room in the east wing had one curved wall and a panelled recess for the sideboard.

Alwington House, once Government House, is now just a memory.

North Kingston

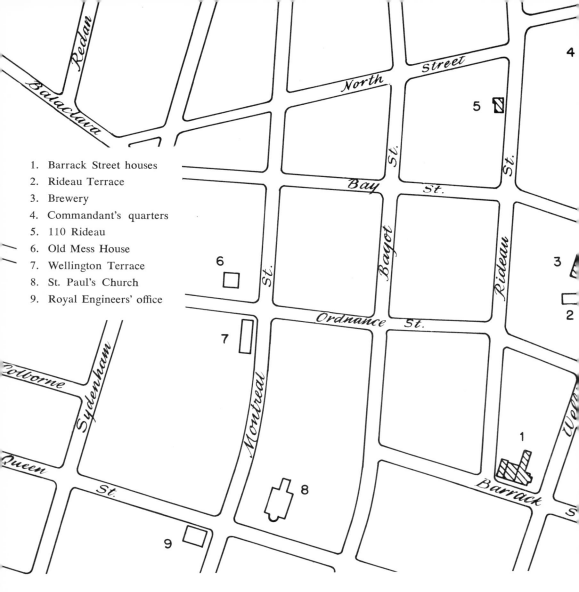

1. Barrack Street houses
2. Rideau Terrace
3. Brewery
4. Commandant's quarters
5. 110 Rideau
6. Old Mess House
7. Wellington Terrace
8. St. Paul's Church
9. Royal Engineers' office

NORTH KINGSTON

MANY OF KINGSTON'S EARLIEST HOMES were in the area along the Cataraqui River, north of Fort Frontenac, where the first settlers chose to build. Rideau Street was at one time the "best" street until Queen Street took precedence. The Commandant's quarters and the Town Major's house were in this section: first on Rideau Street, then on Sydenham on the hill behind the Artillery parade ground.

There were inns and taverns, near the barracks especially. Samuel McGowan kept the Sign of the Royal Oak on Place d'Armes. The Racquet Court Inn on Barrack Street catered to officers, and J. Cochrane had the White Hart Inn near by. On the waterfront there were breweries; in fact, Rideau was once called Brewery Street. Much of the old inner harbour has since been filled in and Rideau Street is no longer near the waterfront.

Defence installations and housing for their personnel dominated this area for many years. The Royal Artillery establishment increased in men and in size and the Tête du Pont Barracks became too small. Richard Cartwright's house, which was on Barrack Street, was taken over in 1814 for officers' quarters. The year before, the Admiralty had bought John Cumming's "elegant stone mansion" on Rideau Street near North, and for some years it was the Commandant's quarters (demolished 1964). Wellington Terrace, at the southwest corner of Montreal and Ordnance streets, was built by Robert Jackson in 1841 to house officers' families. In the same year tenders were called for building an office for the Commander of the Royal Engineers at the southwest corner of Queen and Montreal streets. It is now a hotel, greatly altered.

The earliest Kingston burial ground is on Queen Street at Montreal. Beside it is St. Paul's Anglican Church, built in 1845 in memory of the Reverend Robert David Cartwright. The second burial ground became the site of the present Frontenac Park.

During the 1840–50 period, building extended along Montreal Street to touch the little village of Charlesville, the present Charles and James streets area. On the northwest, houses filled lots from Queen Street to Picardville, the present Division Street and Raglan Road area.

In 1860 a Kingston newspaper reported that the old Mess House at the northwest corner of Montreal and Ordnance was being fitted out for the Sisters of Charity. In 1861 the House of Providence was opened there.

Kingston Brewery

In 1794 a lot was laid out for the Kingston Brewery, and five years later Joseph Forsythe filed a claim to Lot C "on which stands the Kingston Brewery and dwelling house." Lot C is the site of the old stone building with three roof levels on Wellington Street. There is reason to believe that the original Brewery forms part of the present structure. The small cottage on Rideau Terrace, just south of the Brewery, is probably the dwelling that was referred to.

John Darley, who kept the Freemasons' Tavern, operated the Kingston Brewery about 1800. In 1811 John Robins bought the business and it was known as Robins' Brewery until Philip Wenz bought it in 1826. During the thirty-five years that he owned the Brewery it was enlarged, and Jacob Bajus, who bought it in 1861, again added to the building.

The brewers and distillers of those early days were prominent men in the community. The list of those holding licences to operate stills in the Midland District (Kingston and area) in 1803 contained the names of Richard Cartwright, Henry Finkle and William Fairfield. The government had established the earliest saw and grist mills but private enterprise set up the breweries and distilleries.

Today only part of the old building is occupied, but not as a brewery. High in the face of the top storey are two decorative openings holding beer barrels, mute advertisement of a past glory.

99

Barrack Street between Wellington and Rideau

These three houses are typical of many in this area—plain stone buildings crowded on narrow lots. Others that were originally similar have been so altered as to hide their origins, many have burned and some have been torn down to make room for modern buildings.

The double house in the centre is the earliest of the three. It was built by John Mason about 1820. A year later he sold half of it to Robert Duff. The high firewalls at either side, which can be seen at roof level, did not keep it from being badly damaged by fire in 1845.

At the Rideau Street corner David Benson built a narrow house against the double one. His deed is dated 1826. A blocked doorway on the west side of the house is only one of the many alterations which have left little of architectural value.

The big house at the Wellington Street corner was built about 1835 by James Meagher. He had been a member of the 9th Regiment and had settled in Kingston in 1814. His son, Dr. James Meagher, lived in the house and had his surgery there for many years. A house to the east of this was burned in 1845.

The dressed ashlar on the front of the house contrasts sharply with the rubblestone side. The elliptical arched door with panelled reveals also contrasts with the elaborate side porch which was a much later addition.

110 Rideau Street

RESTORED 1975 BY THE FRONTENAC HISTORIC FOUNDATION

This double stone house was at one time the residence of John A. Macdonald, who attained the highest political office in Canada and was knighted by Queen Victoria.

The house was one of several Kingston properties owned by Lieutenant-Colonel Donald Macpherson of the 4th Royal Veterans' Battalion, who was posted to Kingston in 1809 and retired in 1815 to settle here. He had another house at the southwest corner of Bay and Montreal and a third, Cluny House, which stands beside Highway 2, east of Kingston.

Colonel Macpherson's wife was a half-sister of John A.'s mother, Mrs. Hugh Macdonald. Hugh Macdonald brought his family to Kingston from Glasgow, Scotland, in 1820. Here they stayed for a time with the Macphersons, and Hugh Macdonald went into business as a merchant on King Street. His family then lived over his shop. The undertaking failed in a few years, and in 1824 Hugh Macdonald moved his family to Hay Bay and later to Stone Mills to try his hand, still unsuccessfully, at shopkeeping and milling. In 1835, with his wife and two daughters, Margaret and Louisa, he returned to Kingston to live in the south half of the Rideau Street house.

Meanwhile their son, John A., had been in Kingston most of the time, studying law under George Mackenzie. He managed the latter's branch office in Napanee for a year and for a brief time conducted the law office of his cousin, L. P. Macpherson, in Hallowell. Then, in 1835, John A. opened his own office in Kingston. In January 1836 he was admitted to the bar.

The young lawyer was now really the head of the household: his ailing father had but a minor clerkship in a bank; moreover, both Colonel and Mrs. Macpherson were dead and someone had to assume responsibility for their children.

In 1839 the Macdonalds moved from here to a bigger house on Queen Street, the exact location of which has not yet been ascertained.

Though undistinguished architecturally, 110 Rideau Street retains historic interest and distinction by its association with Sir John A. Macdonald, member of Parliament for Kingston, one of the Fathers of Confederation, and first Prime Minister of the Dominion of Canada.

Across the River

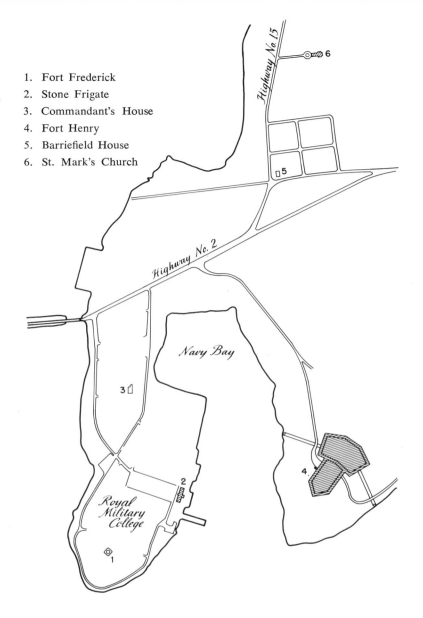

1. Fort Frederick
2. Stone Frigate
3. Commandant's House
4. Fort Henry
5. Barriefield House
6. St. Mark's Church

ACROSS THE RIVER

THE AREA TO THE EAST of the LaSalle Causeway is not legally in the city of Kingston but in terms of history and architecture it is an integral part. Point Frederick was, in fact, at first recommended as the best site for the proposed settlement. On a second look—to consider terrain, exposure of the bay to west winds, and adequate defences—the recommendation was rejected.

From the beginning of British settlement the east side of the Cataraqui River has been associated with defence. A dockyard was established there by the summer of 1789 and a naval base by 1794. With Point Frederick the base of the British navy on Lake Ontario and headquarters of the senior naval officer on the Great Lakes, activity there reached its peak during the War of 1812. And on Point Henry a fort was erected to protect Navy Bay, where warships were built—among them *Royal George*.

When the naval establishment grew, the naval hospital was enlarged, cottages were built for dockyard personnel and a residence was built for the Commodore.

At the same time a village grew up on the hill just beyond government land to serve local residents and defence personnel. The only transportation across the river to Kingston was by ferry until 1826, when the first causeway and toll bridge were built. Richard Cartwright laid out a townsite on some of his land at the top of the hill—the present Barriefield Village. Here were the homes and families of men in the fort and dockyard, and the inns and shops of the suppliers who served them. Barriefield House, at the northeast corner of Highway 15 and James Street, was referred to as an old house in 1834 and was purchased by the government during the First World War. There are many other old stone houses in this little village that is now almost lost in the stream of traffic.

Activity at the naval base declined steadily after the War of 1812, and in order to conform to the Rush-Bagot Agreement of 1817, *St. Lawrence* and various other frigates were laid up. The dockyard was closed in 1834 but hurriedly reopened during the troubles in 1837. Captain Sandom, R.N., was in command, and his men occupied the Stone Frigate.

Fort Frederick was built on the point by 1847, on the site of an earlier blockhouse. It is now operated as a military museum.

The Point Frederick area was revitalized in 1876 when the Royal Military College was established there. From the Stone Frigate the college has expanded to cover the whole peninsula. The present Commandant's House surrounds a few remnants of the Naval Hospital that was built about 1804 and enlarged in 1815. And the defence establishment which started in 1789 at the water's edge now covers hundreds of acres.

St. Mark's Church

BARRIEFIELD VILLAGE

In March 1843, the people of the community were invited to meet at the house of Mr. James Medley "for the purpose of taking into consideration the propriety of erecting a church in the Village of Barriefield." John Bennet Marks, paymaster in the navy, offered a site, and he was made chairman of the building committee. Enough money was subscribed at that first meeting to enable them to proceed immediately. By the end of May they accepted a tender to build according to the plans of Alfred Brunell, Inventor (as the cornerstone names him). His plans have been kept at the church.

When St. Mark's was formally opened in July 1844, it had cost just under £1,000, but its parishioners were spared the inconvenience and expense of crossing the toll bridge to attend church in Kingston.

The original square pews and two-decker pulpit were replaced about 1885. The present chancel was added to the original nave and tower in 1897, and in 1951 the church was completely redecorated. It is a gem of Gothic design; the upward thrust of the fine buttresses is enhanced by the site, which is on a rise beyond the village.

But St. Mark's is now almost surrounded by army property, and the future of the parish is uncertain.

The Stone Frigate

The *Kingston Gazette* of December 16, 1816, had an advertisement which began: "*Government Building*. Wanted to be built, a very substantial stone store house in the Naval Yard at Point Frederick, 200 feet long and 80 feet wide, the roof to be tinned." Three years later the building contract was sent to the Admiralty for approval, and in July 1820 the Naval Storekeeper was authorized to "Hire, on the lowest possible terms, a sufficient number of masons, stonecutters and labourers to complete the said building this summer . . . under the direction of Mr. Fraser, architect, and Officers of the Yard."

The stone, which was quarried on the spot, has a yellow cast very different from the blue-grey Kingston limestone. The three-storey stone building is less than half as big as was first advertised, being 171 feet long and 40 feet wide. Originally, as was intended, it was used to store naval equipment. After the dockyard closed in 1837, the building was used to house some of the men of a naval detachment. They referred to it as their ship and to the floors as decks. From that time on it has been known as the Stone Frigate.

In 1876, when the Royal Military College was established, the Stone Frigate was refitted to become the main college building. Two years later, when the Educational Block was finished, the Stone Frigate became a cadet dormitory, as it is today. The old yellowed stone building on the water's edge stood in sharp contrast to the officers' club along the shore and the large, new, grey limestone buildings on the opposite side of the parade square. But the yellow stone was crumbling and in 1965 to preserve the building it was completely faced with new limestone.

III

Fort Henry

The first Fort Henry was built in 1813 to protect the naval dockyard from attack by land. Plans for a new fort were approved in 1829, as part of a system of defence intended to surround Kingston with five redoubts and a series of martello towers. This plan was not only for the defence of the naval base and military establishment at Kingston but also for the protection of the entrance to the Rideau Canal, which was then being constructed. When the Canal was completed in 1832, the old fort was demolished, and by 1836 the main part of the present Fort Henry was finished. In 1841–42 the Advanced Battery and Commissariat Stores were put up. The other redoubts planned for Kingston were never built, but the martello towers, which were begun in a rush at the time of the Oregon Crisis of 1845, were finished in the following year just after the Oregon Treaty was signed.

Fort Henry was garrisoned by imperial troops up to 1871 and then by Canadians until about 1890, when it was abandoned.

It has never been attacked by an enemy but it has served at times as a prison. John Montgomery, owner of the inn where William Lyon Mackenzie's followers met, was imprisoned in Fort Henry but managed to escape from it. Nils Von Schultz was held there after the Battle of the Windmill and was executed there in 1838. During both world wars German prisoners were interned in Fort Henry.

Today visitors are escorted through the casemates and tunnels by guides who tell the stories of those early prisoners. The Fort Henry Guard, in uniforms of the 1860s, march on the parade ground and fire the ancient cannon on the ramparts according to the drill of that time. On the occasion of an annual ceremonial they also re-enact a battle of the mid-Victorian period. A bit of history thus comes to life as the visitor crosses the drawbridge.

Fort Henry is described by Ronald Way, who supervised its restoration in 1936–38, as a casemated redoubt. The entrance is through the Advanced Battery from the south. The principal part of the fort is surrounded by a dry ditch with access across a drawbridge. Barracks for officers and men are built into the walls of the fort, and the armament, originally twenty-seven cannon, is mounted on the ramparts. There are reverse fire chambers in the counterscarp of the ditch, reached by tunnels from the casemates. Other ditches extend from the moat to martello towers at the shore on either side of the point. Fort Henry, high on the hill, dominates the bay and Point Frederick, and complements the domes and spires of Kingston.

BIBLIOGRAPHY

PRIMARY SOURCES

Cemetery records, Cataraqui and St. Paul's graveyards

Family papers and records privately owned: ANGLIN, loaned by R. W. Anglin; BAXTER, loaned by Isabel Baxter; CARTWRIGHT, loaned by Henry Cartwright; EARL, loaned by Margaret E. Brewster; GRASS, loaned by Donald E. Grass; KIRKPATRICK, loaned by Miss C. M. Morgan; MACPHERSON, loaned by Lt.-Col. J. P. C. Macpherson; MOWAT, loaned by Angus Mowat; STRANGE, loaned by Lt.-Col. Courtland Strange

Frontenac County Registry Office, deeds and records

Kingston City Archives: Assessment rolls, 1839–67; Council minutes; Court of Revision minutes; Petitions to City Council

Ontario Department of Public Records and Archives: Cartwright Papers; Macaulay Papers; Merritt Papers; Stevenson Papers

Parish registers of St. George's Cathedral, Kingston

Public Archives of Canada: Baby Collection; Colonial Office manuscripts; Departmental papers; Correspondence of Governors General; Haldimand Papers; Legislative journals; Macdonald Papers; Ordnance maps; Public Works papers; Secretaries' letter books

Queen's University Archives, Douglas Library: Cartwright Papers; Gildersleeve Papers; Herchmer Papers; Kirby Papers; Kirkpatrick Letter Books; Macaulay Papers; Alexander Morris Papers; Nickle Papers; Trustees' letters and minutes; Walkem documents on fortifications

United Church of Canada Archives, Victoria College, Toronto

Kingston Newspapers, 1810–1900: *Gazette*; *Chronicle*; *Upper Canada Herald*; *Spectator*; *British Whig*; *Chronicle and Gazette*; *News and Chronicle*; *News*; *Argus*

SECONDARY SOURCES

ABELL, WALTER. "An Introduction to Canadian Architecture," *Canadian Geographical Journal* (June 1947)

ADAM, G. MERCER. *The Life and Career of the Rt. Hon. Sir John A. Macdonald* (Toronto, 1891)

ALEXANDER, Sir JAMES E. *L'Acadie, or Seven Years' Explorations in British America* (2 vols., London, 1849)

ANDERSON, ALLAN J. "The Story of St. Mark's" in Kingston Historical Society, *Historic Kingston*, III (1954), 36–40

——— *The Anglican Churches of Kingston* (Kingston, 1963)

ARTHUR, ERIC. *Small Houses of the Late 18th and Early 19th Centuries in Ontario* (Toronto, n.d.)

BONNYCASTLE, Sir RICHARD. *Canada and the Canadians* (London, 1846)

——— *Canada, As It Is, Was, and May Be* (London, 1852)

BRADLEY, A. G. *The United Empire Loyalists* (London, 1932)

BRECK, W. G.; PRESTON, R. A.; and RICHARDSON, F. R. "The Stone Frigate," unpublished MS

BUCKINGHAM, JAMES S. *Canada, Nova Scotia, New Brunswick and the Other British Provinces in North America* (London, 1843)

CALVIN, DELANO DEXTER. *Queen's University* (Kingston, 1941)

——— *Saga of the St. Lawrence* (Toronto, 1945)

——— and GLOVER, T. R. *Corner of Empire* (Cambridge, 1937)

CANNIFF, WILLIAM. *History of Settlement in Upper Canada* (Toronto, 1869)

——— *History of the Province of Ontario* (Toronto, 1872)

CARRUTHERS, J. *Retrospect of 36 Years' Residence in Canada West* (Hamilton, 1861)

CARTWRIGHT, CONWAY, ed., *Letter Book of Hon. Richard Cartwright* (Toronto, 1876)

CARTWRIGHT, Sir RICHARD J. *Reminiscences* (Toronto, 1912)

CHADWICK, E. MARION. *Ontarian Families* (Toronto, 1894–98)

CONNELL, J. C. *History of Kingston General Hospital* (Kingston, 1925)

COOPER, C. W. *Frontenac, Lennox and Addington* (Kingston, 1856)

CREIGHTON, DONALD. *John A. Macdonald* (2 vols., Toronto, 1952, 1955)

CROFTON, W. C. *Sketch of the Life of Metcalfe* (London, 1845)

CRUIKSHANK, ERNEST ALEXANDER. *Settlement of the United Empire Loyalists on the Upper St. Lawrence and Bay of Quinte in 1784* (Toronto, 1934)

CUTTS, ANSON B. "Old Scottish Architecture in Canada," *Canadian Geographical Journal* (Nov. 1949)

DENT, JOHN CHARLES. *The Canadian Portrait Gallery* (Toronto, 1880)

———— *The Last Forty Years* (Toronto, 1881)

———— *Story of the Upper Canada Rebellion* (Toronto, 1885)

DETLOR, GEORGE H. "Diary and Recollections," unpublished MS

DRAPER, W. G. *History of the City* (Kingston, 1862)

———— and SHANNON, W. *Prince of Wales' Visit* (Kingston, 1862)

GIBSON, THOMAS. *Kingston General Hospital* (Kingston, 1935)

GLAZEBROOK, GEORGE P. DE T. *Sir Charles Bagot in Canada* (London, 1929)

———— *A History of Transportation in Canada* (Toronto, 1938)

GOWANS, ALAN. *Looking at Architecture in Canada* (Toronto, 1958)

GUILLET, EDWIN. *Early Life in Upper Canada* (Toronto, 1933, 1963)

———— *The Great Migration* (Toronto, 1937)

———— *Lives and Times of the Patriots* (Toronto, 1938)

———— *Pioneer Inns and Taverns* (Toronto, 1964)

HERRINGTON, WALTER S. "Pioneer Life on the Bay of Quinte" in *Lennox & Addington Historical Society Records*, VI (Napanee)

———— *Pioneer Life among the Loyalists of Upper Canada* (Toronto, 1915)

HINCKS, Sir FRANCIS. *Reminiscences* (Montreal, 1884)

HODGETTS, J. E. *Pioneer Public Service* (Toronto, 1955)

HORSEY, EDWIN. "Kingston," MS in Douglas Library

———— "The Gildersleeves of Kingston," MS in Douglas Library

———— *Kingston a Century Ago* (Kingston, 1938)

JEFFERYS, CHARLES W. *Picture Gallery of Canadian History* (Toronto, 1945)

JENKIN, MABEL. *Historic Kingston and Vicinity* (Kingston, n.d.)

JODOIN, ALEX, and VINCENT, J. *Histoire de Longueuil* (Montreal, 1889)

KEEFER, THOMAS C. *Canals of Canada* (Toronto, 1850)

Kingston Historical Society, *Historic Kingston*, I–XIII (1952–64)

KNAPLUND, PAUL, *Letters from Lord Sydenham to Lord John Russell* (London, 1931)

LA ROCHEFOUCAULD-LIANCOURT, François Alexandre Frédéric, Duc de. *Travels Through the United States of North America, the Country of the Iroquois and Upper Canada* (London, 1799)

LAVELL, W. *History of the Present Fortifications* (Kingston, n.d.)

LOWER, ARTHUR R. M. *Canadians in the Making* (Toronto, 1946)

———— *Colony to Nation* (Toronto, 1958)

McGILL, MARGARET LILY KING. *The Old Limestone City* (Kingston, 1910)

MACHAR, AGNES MAULE. *The Story of Old Kingston* (Toronto, 1908)

MACMECHAN, ARCHIBALD. *The Winning of Popular Government* (Toronto, 1916)

MACPHERSON, J. PENNINGTON. *Life of the Right Hon. Sir John A. Macdonald* (St. John, 1891)

MACRAE, MARION, and ADAMSON, ANTHONY. *The Ancestral Roof* (Toronto, 1963)

MEACHAM, J. H. *Historical Atlas of the Counties of Frontenac, Lennox and Addington* (Toronto, 1878)

MIKEL, W. C. *Some Bay of Quinte Reminiscences* (Belleville, 1922)

MORISON, J. L. *Sir Charles Bagot* (Kingston, 1912)

MUIRHEAD, GEORGE, and STEPHENSON, G. *A Planning Study of Kingston* (Kingston, 1960)

Ontario Historical Society Papers and Records

POPE, JOSEPH. *Memoirs of the Right Honourable Sir John Alexander Macdonald* (Ottawa, 1894)

PRESTON, RICHARD A., ed. *Kingston before the War of 1812* (Toronto, 1959)

———— and LAMONTAGNE, LEOPOLD, eds. *Royal Fort Frontenac* (Toronto, 1958)

Queen's University, Department of History, Masters' theses

READ, DAVID B. *Lives of the Judges of Upper Canada* (Toronto, 1888)

RHYS, Captain HORTON. *A Theatrical Trip to the United States and Canada* (London, 1861)

RICHARDSON, A. J. H. "Biographical Dictionary of Grants," MS

RICHARDSON, Major JOHN. *Eight Years in Canada* (Montreal, 1847)

ROSS, A. E. *History of St. Andrew's Church, Kingston* (Kingston, n.d.)

ROY, JAMES A. *Kingston: The King's Town* (Toronto, 1952)

SCROPE, G. POULETT. *Memoir of the Life of the Rt. Hon. Charles Lord Sydenham* (London, 1843)

SHORTT, ADAM. *Early Records of Courts of Quarter Sessions* (Kingston, 1900)

———— *Lord Sydenham* (Toronto, 1908)

SMITH, W. L. *Pioneers of Old Ontario*, Makers of Canada series

SMITH, WILLIAM HENRY. *Canada: Past, Present and Future* (Toronto, 1851)

STARR, Canon G. L. *Old St. George's* (Kingston, 1913)

STRACHAN, JAMES. *A Visit to the Province of Upper Canada in 1819* (Aberdeen, 1820)

TALMAN, JAMES J. *Loyalist Narratives from Upper Canada* (Champlain Society, 1946)

THOMPSON, EDWARD. *The Life of Charles, Lord Metcalfe* (London, 1937)

TROTTER, REGINALD G. *Canadian Federation* (Toronto, 1924)

VIGER, JACQUES. *Reminiscences of the War of 1812–1814* (Montreal, n.d.)

WALLACE, W. STEWART. *The Family Compact* (Toronto, 1915)

WAY, RONALD. *Old Fort Henry* (1938), reprinted from *Canadian Geographical Journal*

WEAVER, EMILY P. *Story of the Counties of Ontario* (Toronto, 1913)

WHELAN, E. *The Union of the British Provinces* (New York, 1927)

WILSON, G. E. *The Life of Robert Baldwin* (Toronto, 1933)

YOUNG, A. H. *The Rev. John Stuart and Family* (Kingston, 1921)

———— ed., *Parish Register of Kingston, 1784–1811* (Kingston, 1921)

INDEX

ADOLPHUSTOWN, 58
Allen, Grant, 94
Allen, Rev. Joseph A., 94
Alwington House, 37, 92–94
Archbishop's House (Johnson St., next Cathedral), 50
Ardath House, Wolfe Island, 94
Artillery parade ground, 97
Askew, Thomas, 49

BAGOT, Sir CHARLES, 37, 94
Bajus, Jacob, 98
Baker, Henry, 9
Baker, Thomas, 86
Bank of Montreal, 37
Bank of Upper Canada, 19
Barclay, Rev. John, 56
Barrack Street, Nos. 85–89, 100
Barrie Street: No. 18 (Rogers), 73; Nos. 144–146 (Sangster), 73
Barriefield House, 107
Barriefield Village, 107–108
Barrow, R. W., 90
Bay of Quinte, 26
Bay Street Chapel, 9, 68
Beasley, Joanna (Mrs. Richard Cartwright, Sr.), 38
Bell, Rev. William, 56
Bellevue House (35 Centre St.), 30, 62, 84, 86–87
Benson, David, 100
Bethune, Rev. John, 56
Beveridge, J. M. R., 86
Beverley Street: No. 22 (log cottage), 83; No. 86 (Lakeview), 83
Blake, John, 42
Board of Trade, 14, 28, 52
Board of Works, 14
Botsford, Mr., 78
Brant, Molly, 40
Breden, John, 64
Brewery Street (now Rideau), 97
British American Hotel, 19

British American League, 86
British Whig, 90
Brock, Rev. James, 60
Brock Street, No. 251 (Elizabeth Cottage), 54
Browne, George (architect), 20, 30, 49, 56, 76, 78, 83, 92
Brunell, Alfred (architect), 108
Building Society, 52
Butler, Col., 38

CALVIN HOUSE. See Ross
Campbell, Alexander, 52
Carleton Island, 6, 7, 37, 44
Cartwright, John Solomon, 37, 38
Cartwright, Richard, 38, 44, 97, 98, 107
Cartwright, Richard John, 38
Cartwright, Rev. Robert David, 38, 56, 97
Cartwright House (No. 191 King St. East), 38; sketch of doorway, 10
Cedar Island, 15
Centre Street: No. 35 (Bellevue House), 86–87; No. 116 (Otterburn), 83
Charles Place (No. 75 Lower Union St.), 42
Charlesville, 97
Chronicle and News, 15
City Council, 15
City Hall, 19–22, 28, 30, 58, 68, 73
City Park, 46, 58, 60
Clergy Street East, No. 146 (St. Andrew's Manse), 56
Closeburn (No. 5 Emily St.), 90
Cluny House (Highway No. 2), 102
Cochrane, J., 97
Colborne Street, No. 67 (Queen's College), 78
College Street, Nos. 64–66, 32
Collins, John, 19

Commandant of Defence College, 88
Commandant's House, Royal Military College, 107
Commandant's Quarters, 96
Commercial Bank (Empire Life), 37, 44, 52
Commercial Mart (Princess St. at Ontario), 30, 49, 86
Connolly, J. (architect), 50
Counter, John (Mayor), 20, 28, 49, 68, 83
Court of Quarter Sessions, 58
Court House: old, 19, 58; new, 54, 58
Coverdale, William (architect), 20, 54, 68, 73, 83
Crawford, John (architect), 83
Cumming, John, 97
Cunningham, Mrs. Henry, 64
Customs House, 19, 58

DALTON, THOMAS, 83
Darley, John, 98
Dickens, Charles, 19
Dobbs, Harriet (Mrs. R. D. Cartwright), 38
Doyle, Joseph, 60
Doyle's Castle. See McIntosh Castle
Drummond, Robert, 83
Duff, Robert, 100

EARL, ANNE, 40, 49, 62
Earl, Hugh, 40
Earl Place (No. 156 King St. East), 40
Earl Street: No. 53–55, 37; No. 155 (Kerr), 64; No. 161 (Fraser), 64; No. 169 (Machar), 64
Edgehill House, 83
Edgewater (Nos. 1 and 3 Emily St.), 44, 90
Elizabeth Cottage (No. 251 Brock St.), 54

Emily Street: Nos. 1 and 3 (Edgewater), 44, 90; No. 5 (Closeburn), 90
Empire Life (No. 243 King St. East), 37

FAIRFIELD, WILLIAM, 98
Family Compact, 12
Farm Lot No. 24, 73, 79
Farm Lot No. 25, 37, 46, 49
Female Benevolent Society, 76
Ferguson, William (Sheriff), 38, 86
Finkle, Henry, 98
Finkle, Sarah (Mrs. Henry Gildersleeve), 26
Fisher, Alexander, 90
Fisher, Helen (Mrs. Thomas Kirkpatrick), 90
Forsythe, Joseph, 98
Fort Frederick, 107
Fort Frontenac, 6, 7, 96
Fort Henry, 11, 13, 74, 112
Fort Henry Guard, 112
Foster, Lt.-Col. C. L. L., 9, 90
Fowler, Catherine, 54
Fowler, Dr. Fyfe, 54
Fowler, Louisa, 54
Fraser, John, 64
Fraser, Mr. (architect), 110
Freemasons' Tavern, 98
French Church, 50
Frontenac, 26
Frontenac Club (King St. East at William), 37
Frontenac County Court House. *See* Court House
Frontenac Park, 97

GAOL: old, 19; new, 58
Garden Island, 16
Gaulin, Rev. Father Réni, 50
General Hospital. *See* Kingston General Hospital
Gilbert, John, 86
Gildersleeve, Henry, 26
Gildersleeve, Lucretia, 26
Gildersleeve, Overton Smith (Mayor), 26
Glover, Dr. W. R., 26
Gore Street: No. 59 (Stuart Cottage), 78; Nos. 89–91, 37

Government House, 92
Governor General, 13, 14, 37, 88, 92
Grant, Caroline Coffin, 92
Grant, Charles James Irwin, 94
Grant, Charles William, 92
Grant, Charlotte (Mrs. Joseph A. Allen), 94
Grant, David Alexander, 92
Grant, William, 64
Grass, Michael, 46, 49

HAGERMAN, CHRISTOPHER, 90
Hales, Charles, 30, 32, 49, 84, 86
Hales Cottages (Nos. 311–317 King St. West), 84
Hallowell, 102
Hamilton, Clark, 44
Hamilton, John, 44
Hamilton, Peter Hunter, 44
Hamilton, Robert, 44
Hardy, Edward H., 62
Harper, Francis, 83
Hawthorne Cottage (St. Mary's of the Lake), 83
Hay Bay, 102
Herchmer, Jane, 44
Herchmer, Lawrence, 19
Herchmer, Mary (Mrs. Robert Hamilton), 44
Hill, Francis Manning, 83
Hillcroft (No. 26 Hillcroft Crescent), 83
Horsey, Edward (architect), 54, 58, 60
Horsey, Elizabeth (Mrs. Fyfe Fowler), 54
Hospital: cholera, 44; naval, 107. *See also*: Hôtel Dieu; Kingston General; Ontario Hospital
Hôtel Dieu, 49, 50
House of Providence (Old Mess House), 97

Inkerman, 60

JACKSON, ROBERT, 97
James Street, Barriefield, 107
Jamieson, Robert, 28
Johnson, Sir John, 48, 73
Johnson, Sir William, 40

Johnson Street: Nos. 178–180 (Askew), 49; at Clergy (St. Mary's Cathedral), 50; Nos. 228–230 (Mowat), 52

KERR, JOHN, 64
Kerr, Johnson B. W., 40
King Street East: No. 53 (Murney House), 46; Nos. 131–133, 37; No. 156 (Earl Place), 40; No. 191 R. D. Cartwright), 38; No. 203 (Knaresborough), 37; No. 221 (J. S. Cartwright), 37; corner of William (Frontenac Club), 37; at Johnson (St. George's Cathedral), 24; No. 243 (Empire Life), 37; No. 264 (Gildersleeve), 26
King Street West: Nos. 311–317 (Hales Cottages), 84; No. 355 (Hawthorne Cottage), 83; No. 440 (St. Helen's), 90
Kingston Brewery, 98
Kingston Gas Company, 52
Kingston General Hospital, 11, 13, 73, 76, 78, 84, 92
Kingston Historical Society, 74
Kingston Mills, 11
Kingston Waterworks Company, 15
Kirkpatrick, George Airey (Sir), 90
Kirkpatrick, Thomas (Mayor), 44, 90
Knaresborough Cottage (No. 203 King St. East), 37

LAKEVIEW (No. 86 BEVERLEY ST.), 83
LaSalle Causeway, 106
Laura Secord. *See* Mowat's Round Corner Building
Law Society of Upper Canada, 42
Lewis, Rev. J. Travers, 24
Log cottage (No. 22 Beverley St.), 83
Longueuil, Baroness de, 92

118

Lower Union Street, No. 75 (Charles Place), 42

MACAULAY, ANN, 37
Macaulay, John, 19, 73
Macdonald, Hugh, 102
Macdonald, Isabella, 86
Macdonald, Sir John A., 15, 28, 49, 52, 86, 102
Macdonald, Louisa, 102
Macdonald, Margaret, 102
Macdonell, Rev. Father Alexander (Bishop), 48, 50
McDowall, Rev. Robert, 56
McGowan, Samuel, 97
Machar, Agnes Maule, 64
Machar, Rev. John, 56, 64
Machar House (No. 169 Earl St.), 64
McIntosh, Donald, 60
McIntosh Castle (No. 14 Sydenham St.), 60
McKay & Redpath, 11
Mackenzie, George, 102
Mackenzie, William Lyon, 112
Macklem House. See Rogers House
McLean, Allan, 42
Maclean House. See Murney House
McLeod House. See Cartwright House
Macpherson, Lt.-Col. Donald, 102
Macpherson, Frances (Mrs. John Hamilton), 44
Macpherson, L. P., 102
Market Battery, 15
Market Street hotels, 19
Marks, John Bennet, 108
Martello towers, 15, 74, 112
Mason, John, 100
Masonic Temple, 68
Meagher, James, 100
Medley, James, 108
Metcalfe, Sir Charles, 19, 20, 37, 94
Military Headquarters (St. Helen's), 83, 90
Miller, Colin, 40
Milner, James, 49
Moira, 40
Molson, Thomas, 83

Montague Place. See Earl Place
Montgomery, John, 112
Montreal Street at Ordnance (Wellington Terrace), 97
Morton, James, 83, 90
Mortonwood (St. Helen's), 90
Mowat, Catharine (Mrs. John Fraser), 64
Mowat, George L., 32, 52
Mowat, John, 30, 32, 52, 64
Mowat, Rev. John Bower, 52
Mowat, Oliver, 52
Mowat Houses (Nos. 228–230 Johnson St.), 52
Mowat's Round Corner Building (Princess St. at Bagot), 30, 32, 52
Murney, Mrs. Henry, 44, 46, 49
Murney House (No. 53 King St. East), 46
Murney Tower (King St. at Barrie), 74
Muscovado Cottage. See Bellevue House
Muscovy Mansion. See Bellevue House

NAPANEE, 102
Naval Hospital, 107
Navy Bay, 107
Newcourt (King St. West), 30
Newlands, George, 58
Newlands, William, 50
Nickalls, James, Jr., 42
Nickle Wing, Kingston General Hospital, 76
North Gate, 9
North Street cottage. See Commandant's Quarters

OLD ARTS BUILDING, QUEEN'S, 78
Old Medical, Queen's, 78
Old Mess House (House of Providence), 97
Oldfield, Col., 14
Oliver, Ann Louisa (Mrs. Nickalls), 42
Oliver, Charles, 42
Oliver, George, 42
Ongwanada (St. Helen's), 90

Ontario Hospital, 68
Ontario Street: at Johnson (Plymouth Square), 28; at Market (Herchmer), 19; No. 253 (Macaulay), 19
Orange Arch Incident, 90
Oregon Crisis, 74, 112
Otterburn (No. 116 Centre St.), 83

PANZERONI, 50
Parliament, 13, 76
Parliament Building, 13, 46, 76, 78, 84, 92
Paton, Mrs. Isabella Hamilton, 48
Pekoe Pagoda. See Bellevue House
Penitentiary, 11, 54, 68, 84, 88
Pense, Edward John Barker, 90
Picardville, 97
Plaza Hotel. See Royal Engineers' Office
Plymouth Square (Ontario St. at Johnson), 28
Point Frederick, 9, 106–107, 110, 112
Post Office, 19, 20
Power, John (architect), 60
Power, Joseph (architect), 24
Prince George Hotel (Herchmer House), 19
Prince of Wales, 90
Princess Street: No. 27 (Commercial Mart), 30; at Bagot St. (Round Corner), 30, 32; Nos. 320–322 (Weeks), 78
Princess Street United Church, 68

QUEEN STREET METHODIST CHURCH, 68
Queen Victoria, 102
Queen's College and University, 14, 32, 44, 49, 52, 56, 64, 78, 83, 86, 88

RACQUET COURT INN, 97
Rear Street. *Now* Bagot
Rebellion of 1837, 12, 76, 112

Rees, Mrs. Edgerton (Grace Hardy), 62
Regiopolis College, 49, 50
Registry Office, 58
Richardson, Senator Henry W., 94
Richardson Building (Macaulay), 19
Rideau Canal, 11, 74, 112
Rideau Street, No. 110 (J. A. Macdonald), 102
Rideau Terrace, 98
Robertson, George, & Sons, 28
Robins, John, 98
Rochefoucauld-Liancourt, Duc de la, 8
Rogers, Thomas (architect), 24, 73, 76
Rogers House (No. 18 Barrie St.), 73
Roode, Catharine Burnett, 28
Roode, Hannah (Mrs. John Counter), 28
Roode, Harvey, 28
Roselawn (Union St. at College), 88
Rosemount (No. 48 Sydenham St.), 62
Ross, Charles, 73
Round Corner Building (Princess St. at Bagot), 30, 32, 52
Royal Artillery, 97
Royal Canadian Rifles, 16
Royal Engineers, 14, 74; office, 97
Royal George, 40, 107
Royal Military College, 9, 24, 107, 110
Royal Veterans' Battalion, 102
Russell, Lord John, 13
Ryerson, Rev. Egerton, 68

S & R Store. See Commercial Mart
St. Andrew's Church, 52, 56, 78
St. Andrew's Manse (146 Clergy St. East), 56
St. George's Cathedral (King St. East at Johnson), 9, 24, 38, 50, 56, 92

St. Helen's (440 King St. West), 90
St. James Anglican Church, 68, 73
St. James of Boanarges Chapel, 50
St. Joseph's Church, 50
St. Lawrence, 107
St. Mark's Church (Barriefield), 108
St. Mary's Cathedral (Johnson St. at Clergy), 50
St. Mary's of the Lake (Hawthorne Cottage), 83
St. Paul's Church, 97
Sandom, Capt., 107
Sangster, Charles, 73
Scobell, Richard, 19
Scobell & Tossell, 58
Secord, Magdalen (Mrs. Richard Cartwright, Jr.), 38
Selma Park, 48
Shaw, Samuel, 64
Sign of the Royal Oak, 97
Simcoe, Governor and Mrs., 7
Sisters of Charity, 97
Sisters of the Religious Hospitallers of St. Joseph, 49
Smith, David John, 88
Smith, Henry, Sr. and Jr., 88
Smith, Peter, 88
South Roode Cottage (Sunnyside), 83
Stewart, James (architect), 49
Stinson, Rev. Joseph, 68
Stone Frigate, 9, 107, 110
Stone Mills, 102
Store Street. Now Princess
Strange, Dr. Orlando, 40
Stuart, Archdeacon George Okill, 24, 37, 56, 73, 78
Stuart, Rev. John, 7, 24, 73, 78
Stuart Cottage (No. 59 Gore St.), 78
Stuart's Folly (Summerhill), 78
Stuartsville, 78
Summerhill (Queen's Campus), 78

Sunnyside (Union St. West), 83
Sydenham, Lord, 13, 24, 83, 84, 92
Sydenham Street: No. 14 (McIntosh Castle), 60; No. 48 (Rosemount), 62
Sydenham Street Church, 28, 68

Teacaddy Castle. See Bellevue House
Tête du Pont Barracks, 24, 97
Thomson, Charles Poulett. See Sydenham, Lord
Town Council, 14
Town Major, 96

Union Street West: near Macdonell (South Roode Cottage, now Sunnyside), 83; at College (Roselawn), 88
United Empire Loyalists, 6

Victoria & Grey Trust Co. See Wilson's Buildings
Von Schultz, Nils, 112

Walker, Edward and Robert, 19
War of 1812, 8, 74, 107
Watkins Wing, General Hospital, 76
Way, Ronald, 112
Weeks, Hiram, 78
Wellington Street, No. 168 (Wilson's Buildings), 30
Wellington Terrace (Montreal St. at Ordnance), 97
Wells & Thompson (architects), 76
Wenz, Philip, 98
White Hart Inn, 97
William Street: No. 185 (Stewart), 49; No. 207 (Browne), 49
Williamsville, 68
Wilson, James, 86
Wilson, William Henry, 30
Wilson's Buildings (No. 168 Wellington St.), 30
Wolfe Island, 7, 94
Worsley, Col. P. W., 86
Wulff, Lt.-Col. Henry P., 86